Eleven Authors
In Search
Of a Building

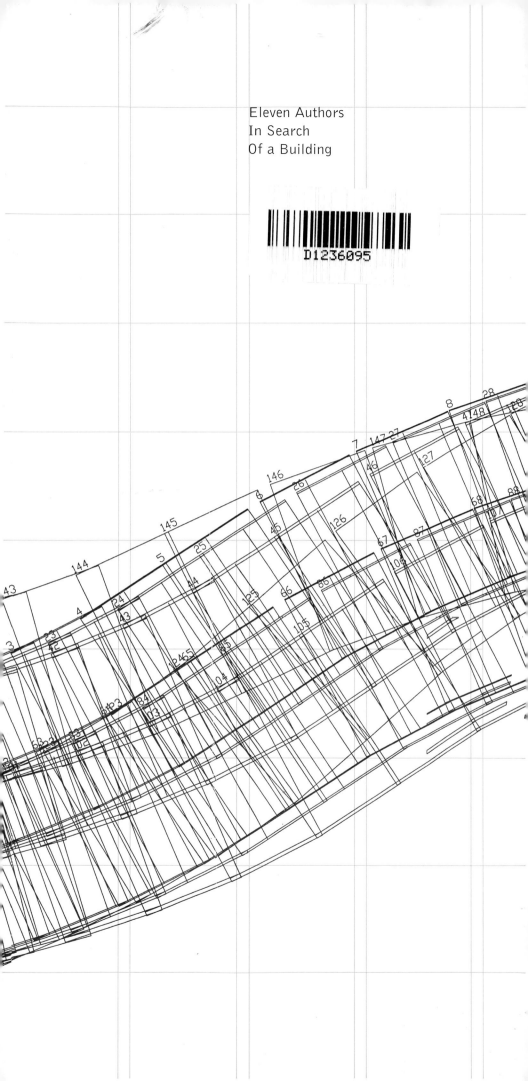

The Aronoff
Center for
Design and Art
at the
University of Cincinnati

Design by
Pentagram

The Monacelli Press

Eleven Authors
In Search
Of a Building

A building by
Eisenman Architects
A book edited by
Cynthia C. Davidson

Library of Congress Cataloging-in-Publication Data:
Eleven authors in search of a building: the Aronoff Center for Design and Art at the University of Cincinnati / a building by Eisenman Architects; a book edited by Cynthia C. Davidson.

p.   cm.

ISBN 1-885254-45-8 (pbk.)

1. Eisenman, Peter, 1932– —Criticism and interpretation. 2. Aronoff Center for Design and Art. 3. Eisenman Architects. 4. Deconstructivism (Architecture)— Ohio—Cincinnati. 5. Cincinnati (Ohio)— Buildings, structures.

I. Davidson, Cynthia C. II. Eisenman Architects.

NA737.E33E43 1997
720′.92—dc20   96 - 34532

First published in the United States of America in 1996 by The Monacelli Press, Inc.
10 East 92nd Street
New York, New York 10128

Copyright © 1996 The Monacelli Press, Inc., and the College of Design, Architecture, Art, and Planning, University of Cincinnati

Printed and bound in the United States of America

Designed by Pentagram

Cover photo by Jeff Goldberg/ESTO

ACKNOWLEDGMENTS

There would be no Eleven Authors in Search of a Building were it not for the building that inspired the search, the Aronoff Center for Design and Art at the University of Cincinnati, and for the people who made completion of this project by Eisenman Architects possible: University of Cincinnati President Joseph A. Steger; Dean Jay Chatterjee of the College of Design, Architecture, Art, and Planning; and State Senator Stanley J. Aronoff, for whom this building is named in recognition of his support for the University and the project.

There also would be no book if not for the authors who made a trip to Cincinnati, some from great distances, just to visit the Aronoff Center and to take on the challenge of writing about it. Production of the book was only possible with the beyond-the-call-of-duty assistance of two architects, Richard Rosson, associate-in-charge of the building, and Donna Barry, a project architect. Their attention to design documentation, drawings, coordinate geometry, and photographs made possible the details that both the search for this building and the design of this book required. Daniel S. Friedman, an assistant professor at the University of Cincinnati, provided margin notes, and Thomas de Monchaux and Juliette Cezzar, editorial assistants in New York, checked every coordinate dimension and comma. The generous support and tireless efforts of Bob Ott, Sr., and Bob Ott, Jr., at The Hennegan Printing Company made possible the production of the book on a very short deadline. Mead Paper made a generous donation of paper. Finally, Michael Bierut and Esther Bridavsky (both University of Cincinnati alumni) of the New York graphic design studio Pentagram created a design that acts as a kind of oblique mirror to the building, pulling the eye in as many directions and to as much information as does the Aronoff Center itself. — CCD

TABLE
OF
CONTENTS

SIGNATURE OF EXCELLENCE

Joseph A. Steger

President

University of Cincinnati

The newly completed Aronoff Center for Design and Art is a signature of excellence that confirms the rebirth of the physical environment at the University of Cincinnati.

In 1989 we identified the need to unify our two principal campuses and to build approximately one million square feet of new academic and research space. Working with world-renowned landscape architect George Hargreaves of San Francisco, and with the assistance of Dale McGirr, vice president for finance for the University, and Jay Chatterjee, dean of the College of Design, Architecture, Art, and Planning, we began to develop a Master Plan to guide this effort. After significant consultation with faculty, staff, students, and trustees, we concluded that the development of our physical campus should create links between the East and West Campuses, between academic disciplines, and between the University and its surrounding community.

We decided to use open space as the primary organizing element, with buildings clustered around central gathering places, and vowed to affirm and honor the University's tradition of diversity, both in its academic organization and in its student body. We decided to encourage students of all ages to live on campus, providing them with an opportunity for lifelong learning. Finally, we promised to take advantage of the unique qualities of the University — its varied physical landscape, the round-the-clock nature of its campus life, and the multidisciplinary approach of its constituent colleges.

An important enhancement to the Master Plan was our idea to increase appreciation of our campus through signature buildings created by the best, brightest, and most accomplished architects working today. I am pleased to say that with the completion of the Aronoff Center for Design and Art we have accomplished all of these goals — and more. Today, the University of Cincinnati is the only campus where five architects of international stature have major projects in simultaneous development. In addition to Peter Eisenman, designer of the Aronoff Center for Design and Art, architects working on signature buildings conceived under the original Master Plan are David Childs, Henry Cobb, Frank Gehry, and Michael Graves.

The University of Cincinnati has always been much more than just brick and mortar. We represent a collection of some of the most extraordinary academic and research talent found anywhere in the world. We are proud to be among the top 75 research institutions, ranked by the Carnegie Commission from the 5,000 colleges and universities of the United States. We are truly a global institution. The University of Cincinnati attracts students from more than eighty-five countries every year. We have sister-university agreements in twenty-three countries, and our faculty conduct research or teach in more than one hundred countries. Equally significant, the use and impact of new media technology on educational processes continue to be revealed. Yet even as we move to a university without walls, we cannot escape the reality that a first-rank university needs proper facilities to thrive.

The Aronoff Center for Design and Art provides us with a setting conducive to grand achievement. It is a physical environment that inspires and challenges us to greatness in our endless quest to expand and harness the intellect. We are deeply and eternally grateful to State Senator Stanley J. Aronoff, without whom this project would never have become a reality, and to the tens of thousands of people whose support and generosity make a degree from the University of Cincinnati a signature of excellence throughout the world.

GATEWAY TO THE FUTURE

Jay Chatterjee

Dean

College of Design, Architecture, Art, and Planning

University of Cincinnati

THE PROGRAM OF THE ARONOFF CENTER WAS TO REORGANIZE THE EXISTING 145,000 SQUARE FEET OF THE COLLEGE OF DESIGN, ARCHITECTURE, ART, AND PLANNING (DAAP), HOUSED IN A CLUSTER OF THREE BUILDINGS FROM THE 1950S AND '70S, AND TO BUILD AN ADDITIONAL 150,000 SQUARE FEET OF EXHIBITION, LIBRARY, THEATER, STUDIO, AND OFFICE SPACE, THEREBY CREATING A FACILITY THAT UNIFIES THE FOUR SCHOOLS OF THE COLLEGE.

From their first moment, visitors to the new Aronoff Center for Design and Art are inspired by its energetic expression of the human spirit and its quest for knowledge and achievement. In a world of too many virtual realities, it is a physical space that expands our boundaries and establishes new limits for the possible. Imagination and innovation, fully realized, envelop us and remind us that our reach should exceed our grasp.

As a college of design, architecture, art, and planning, we constantly seek new ways to express our disciplines and force them to stretch and grow. With Peter Eisenman as architect, we have done exactly that — created an extraordinary building that serves as a point of departure for the theory and practice of architecture. It is a design and vision that soars in its eloquence.

The Aronoff Center brings together, for the first time, all of the University of Cincinnati's design-oriented programs into a single, unified complex. The Center functions as a signature gateway to the University of Cincinnati campus. It is a new landmark at the corner where most people enter the University, and where the vast majority of our visitors get their first view of the campus. The project consists of 304,000 square feet of new and renovated space for the College of Design, Architecture, Art, and Planning (DAAP), including teaching, research, and exhibition space.

The College of Design, Architecture, Art, and Planning is unique in that it brings together four major schools under a single roof. Very few universities offer this concentration of disciplines in a single college. The most important element of the Aronoff Center is a vast concourse running the length of the new construction — a multipurpose connecting space that serves as a metaphorical living room for the College. This space facilitates interaction and collaboration among the different disciplines in the College, and serves as a place for people to meet, mingle, and eat together. It is directly connected to the major academic centers of the College as well as the exhibition gallery and state-of-the-art computer graphics center.

The design of the building contributes to the theory and practice of architecture on many different levels. When one is inside, it continually challenges the senses and fools the eye. Space expands and contracts, always presenting a changing aspect as one looks from one area to another. In a conventional building, one walks down an institutional corridor, lined with office and classroom doorways. The interior of the Aronoff Center meets the same programmatic requirement, but in the process it twists and torques through the building, turning the mere act of walking "down the hall" into a thoroughly engaging experience.

The Aronoff Center, like all of the new buildings constructed under the University of Cincinnati's Master Plan, is also sensitive to its surroundings, fitting into the cityscape and creating a smooth transition from campus to city and back again. The building hugs its hilly site and fits in naturally with the city park across the street. It is environmentally responsible — efficient to operate and economical to heat and cool. The existing Alms, DAAP, and Wolfson buildings are integrated beautifully with the Aronoff addition, working together as a single complex. We have succeeded in showing respect for what was built before while aggressively moving ahead into the future. In function and form, in attitude and execution, in spirit and substance, the Aronoff Center symbolizes the essence and raison d'être of a great University — it is our Gateway to the Future.

DAAP'S FOUR SCHOOLS (DESIGN, ARCHITECTURE AND INTERIOR DESIGN, ART, AND PLANNING) CONTAIN 10 UNDERGRADUATE AND SEVEN GRADUATE PROGRAMS WITH A TOTAL OF 1,500 UNDERGRADUATE STUDENTS AND 240 GRADUATE STUDENTS. THERE ARE 92 FULL-TIME FACULTY AND 28 PART-TIME FACULTY.

INTRODUCTION

Cynthia C. Davidson

When one follows the design and production of a building for nearly nine years, it is natural to have preconceptions about the built outcome, to anticipate certain qualities in the three-dimensional experience of its space. The Aronoff Center for Design and Art, an Eisenman Architects' project for the College of Design, Architecture, Art, and Planning (DAAP) at the University of Cincinnati, is such a building. Throughout its long development, many opportunities to look at the drawings, plans, and models of the building presented themselves — an exhibition of the project at the Fifth International Architecture Biennale in Venice in 1991 and a show at the Contemporary Arts Center in Cincinnati the following year gave thousands of viewers a preview of the building to come. A <u>Progressive Architecture</u> design award (1991) and numerous other published versions of the project made it seem a reality — something that elicited a reaction, if not physical then mental — long before ground was broken for construction in October 1993. It was, in fact, so exposed, so well-known, and so effectively criticized before its realization as a built work, that one had to stop and think, "What is the actual status of this project?" for it already, through these screens of mediation, seemed real beyond its being.

This early exposure of the Aronoff Center provided the authors in this book with many opportunities to have certain preconceptions about the project. From the beginning I expected this to be an unusual building, perhaps the most interesting and complex one the office had done. The long, sinuous curve of the addition, worming its way into or out of an earthen hill and slithering alongside the orthogonal geometry of the original DAAP buildings, posed more conceptual problems than anything the office had previously attempted, seemingly defying traditional conceptions of plan and section. In spite of our familiarity with the project, the building itself still challenged us to find a way to understand its "defiance."

Go to presentation model page 102

Having been weaned on the American modernism based on the Miesian and Le Corbusian academies, I learned to think about a building first from its plan and only later in section. Equally, my experience of Italian Renaissance buildings and the writings of Colin Rowe taught me to expect some form of promenade architecturale as a way of introducing the experiencing subject into a critical understanding of a building. Initially, the plan depiction of the Aronoff Center's sinuous form did suggest the possibility of a promenade architecturale, one climbing a hill and providing a route that gives the subject continuously unfolding views. Other drawings, however, suggested that this promenade might be complicated — if not the route itself, then the view of the moving subject — or even that the promenade might be compromised, thereby presenting a false analogue for understanding the building. This was hinted at in the incredibly dense yet lacelike wireframe drawings that appeared and reappeared in the explanations of the plans, sections, and construction process. Additionally, the architects talked of chevrons and x-y-z coordinates, of segmented lines, asymptotic tilts, and torquing of all kinds. These uncommon terms in architecture and these unusual drawings that only a computer program, no human hand, could endlessly draw and redraw suggested too the possibility that no previous conception such as the promenade architecturale would account for the experience of the built space that would result.

Go to
wireframe
page 38

Go to
500 Level NC Coordinate Dimension Plan
page 90

Throughout the early months of 1996, the authors asked to write about the Aronoff Center for this book began to visit the nearly completed building. In a sense they were asked to explain their experiences of the building in terms of their own theoretical discourses, but it is clear from the frustrations that inhibit their writing that the building indeed thwarts conventional explanations. Each critic here brings a different perspective on architecture to the building, but the building itself (and its chief designer, Peter Eisenman, as well) refuses to work within these categories of knowledge. It is not simply a building, an object on a landscape, but a work of architecture that, through the process of its making and then the shape this process takes, challenges the conventions of architectural theory, typology, history, program, production — all of the issues that the authors here address.

Still I did not visit the building. Then photographs of the Center began to arrive, and gradually the sinuous form that I had expected to be dominant was strangely compromised. The exterior, so strong in bird's-eye view, was from the pedestrian's perspective no longer apparent. Photographs of the interior seemed to reveal space compressing and expanding in ways that were impossible to fully understand in a still image. So on June 19, 1996, with the informational baggage of drawings and photographs and the essays for this book, and with the finished building declared open for occupancy, I went to see the Aronoff Center.

Arriving by car with Dean Jay Chatterjee, the first thing I noticed is that indeed there is no facade, no outside to speak of. This condition, noted by several authors here, gave me a clue about what I was to see. For in reality, on the site, the exterior of the building is more fragmented than the early drawings and models had led me to expect. The visitor, repeating patterns discerned by Bertolt Brecht, constructs this object: "[T]he relation of form to content is no longer a relation to exteriority, the form resembling clothes which can dress no matter what content, it is process, genesis, result of a work." This notion of process would continue to reveal itself throughout the building. After parking in the adjacent garage, I walked a short distance to what is called the lower or 300 level entrance, marked by a dramatic hammerhead form that looms over and illuminates this grade-level entry. This is not so much a formal entry as a wedge of space, and the feeling is subterranean due to the cover provided by the steps and platforms leading to the 400 level entrance above. Because this ceiling blocks any other view of the building, the hammerhead gains even greater importance, its form seeming to force open the wedge between the new and old buildings. Here I feel constricted, caught in a vertical compression of space. A gridded panel of fluorescent lighting that floats on the bottom of the hammerhead continues into the lobby, pulling me into the building Once inside, the compression dissipates, albeit in another double-height space that pulls my eye in several directions, spilling into corridors and doorways. Overhead a bridge acts as a dam and a filter but gives no indication of which way I am to go. In fact, there is no sign of traditional circulation, no marche, no promenade architecturale.

Go to
facade view
page 66

Go to
entrance view
page 20

Cited in Gregory Ulmer, "The Object of Post-Criticism," in The Anti-Aesthetic: Essays on Postmodern Culture, ed. Hal Foster (Seattle: Bay Press, 1983), 86.

In an attempt to find this elusive promenade I decided to reexperience entry from the 400 level. The quickest way up is through the 350-seat auditorium, where other kinds of clues about the building appear: overhead a chevron colored pale green and marked with fluorescent tubing cranks across the ceiling; walls torque and change color and a balcony runs along one side. I climb the slope of the hall and enter a windowed corridor that leads to the auditorium from the 400 level.

Coming onto the 400 level, I turn left to exit and then reenter the building through its main entrance. Though one level higher than before, I am still in the "same" space, but here it is compressed horizontally, pushed against the same ceiling as below. This compression, so different from the vertical slot of the 300 level space below, creates the sensation of shearing. Again there is no idea of sequence and continuity, only the feeling of cutting and difference. The main stair that, according to the information I know so well, should lead me through the form of the building is nowhere to be seen. Instead, looking around I see other routes: to my left, a chevron I can walk on — that crosses over the 300 level lobby and connects the Aronoff to an old DAAP building; ahead, another channel of space; and finally, to my right, tucked behind a cascading wall, the so-called main stair, the height and length of which I can only imagine through the compression of space in front of me. But which way to go? The "main stair," called College Hall, does not pull with importance the way the channel does. I follow the channel to what is suddenly a three-story sky-lit space, oddly triangular in shape. This is the College cafe. Though soaring in scale, it seems to be something left over, a residue of the main energies of the building. It is also, I discover, quite by accident, where a stair from the 300 level does in fact reach the 400 level. From its beginning this route is interrupted, causing anyone who uses the stair to cross the cafe and double back to reach the main stair, which is also always hidden from view. This disruptive break in the promenade suggests other breaks from traditionally thought typologies. Something other is emerging.

Was it in the cafe, sipping coffee, that I first noticed it? Not just the ability to see, but the uncanny feeling of being seen as well? Disembodied heads bob along a 500 level chevron bridge that crosses above; at the

THE AGONISTIC INTENSITY OF THE COMPOSITION OVERWHELMS THE WEAKNESS OF INDIVIDUAL MATERIAL PROPERTIES. THE SUBJECT OF THE BUILDING IS NOT THE MATERIAL OF CONSTRUCTION; THE MATERIAL OF THE BUILDING IS THE CONSTRUCTION OF THE SUBJECT. THE BUILDING PROVIDES AN APANOPTICAL HOUSING FOR PANOPTICAL INSTITUTIONS. IT CONFRONTS SCHOOLS OF PLANNING, ART, DESIGN, AND ARCHITECTURE (INDEED, THE WHOLE UNIVERSITY), WITH WHAT JOAN COPJEC, IN READ MY DESIRE, CALLS "NON-KNOWLEDGE" AND "INVISIBILITY." TO BE SURE, COPJEC WRITES ABOUT FILM THEORY'S MISDIAGNOSIS OF THE PANOPTIC GAZE. STILL, TO THE EXTENT THAT ANY ARCHITECTURE CAN ANNUL ITS OWN KNOWLEDGE AND VISIBILITY, THIS BUILDING EDGES UP TO COMPARABLY EXTREME LIMITS, "UNDERMINING EVERY CERTAINTY," OPENING ITS INHABITANTS TO THE "INCOMPLETENESS OF EVERY MEANING AND POSITION."
— D.F.

Go to auditorium view page 132

Go to 400 Level panorama page 158

Go to
chevron bridge view
page 124

Go to
stair view
page 144

Go to
view from gallery
page 150

narrow end of the cafe, where the walls compress the high space to a point, voices float down from an unseen place of observation. Not only does space eddy and flow but I am aware of the uncanny presence of people whose bodies, distant from mine, drift in and out of view as they move through the building.

I double back to College Hall and begin to climb the main stair. This is familiar, not just from the plan but also from the ramp in Eisenman's Wexner Center for the Visual Arts and the concourse in the Greater Columbus Convention Center, two buildings that are basically circulation spines. But here, as one author describes, the route through the building never visually divulges its end, which, unlike the Wexner Center and Convention Center, means that the circulation no longer allows one to conceptualize the building as a whole. Rather, understanding comes in fragments. The movement up and across the wide platforms, like the twisting exterior stair leading to the 400 level entry, presents opportunities to deviate, to stop, even to lose the idea of destination. When I stop to look back down the stair I cannot see where I began. In fact, the building seems to shift, as again wall planes and cuts, torques and slots present no single view but rather views of other views and views through the space that are not panoptic but are cut. This sensation of movement and change suggests that a new way of understanding this building must be found.

If one thinks of another building in which the body of the subject and the object merge, such as the Guggenheim Museum in New York, the experience is still within what can be called a panoptic view. But the movement and activity of bodies in the space of the Aronoff Center enact a process akin to that of filmic montage, in which one frame of a film is propelled into and upon the next frame. In this sense, montage is an alternative to an organic model, such as the promenade and its classic ideas of linearity and closure. In the context of architecture, montage would not be expected to reproduce the real, but to construct a process/object "not to reflect but to change reality."

Ibid.

On the 500 level, the chevron bridge that overlooks the cafe leads to an art gallery that overlooks an area that abuts a former DAAP building exterior wall, the windows of which now look into the Center. Everything is looking, watching, but discretely, perhaps even

Go to
300 Level view
page 113

unknowingly. Views unfold and then dissolve one into another as quickly as I move my eye. Through the cuts in the building I see fragments of bodies — legs without torsos, torsos without heads, and find myself watching, waiting for the building to reveal more. To watch, the building forces me to move, pushing me through the space in search of a better view, another perspective from which I can enhance my role not just as the viewing subject, but as a voyeur. Here the idea of montage suddenly collapses into the idea of the subject as voyeur, simultaneously watching and watched.

In the Renaissance, the ideal object mirrored the ideal subject. In modern architecture, the subject reconstitutes the object. In the Aronoff Center, the object is not activated by the subject; rather, the object defines the subject by fracturing the subject as both seen and seeing — in one sense, the subject itself becomes a montage. The subject becomes enfolded in the experience of the object, in the fracturing of space that then fractures the bodies glimpsed in space, reflecting that the subject is also being seen as a fractured condition. This suggests that the process of montage can replace the traditional architectural narrative, the promenade architecturale, as a way of explaining the building, as a way of explaining the fractured double subject/object in a new interior landscape.

As the interior of the Aronoff Center looks back at the subject and forces the subject to look, to begin to watch, not just for the changing forms of the building itself but also for the framing and reframing of the subject him or herself, the role of the subject/critic comes into question. This is a new kind of spatial experience for the subject, one that suggests a search not just for a building and the theoretical frameworks that might explain it, but also a repositioning of the subject. For here, theory, the privileged apparatus of the subject/critic, no longer serves to frame the building. Rather, the building frames theory, shattering the preconceptions formed during its making and pushing at the limitations of theory — and of this book — as well. It is a building that demands more than thinking or viewing; it demands the simultaneous experience of both.

Cynthia C. Davidson is a co-founder and editor of ANY magazine and editor of the 11-volume series of books based on the Anyone architecture conferences, including Anyone, Anywhere, Anyplace, Anywise, and Anyway.

x=521.17
y=171.09
z=785.50

Go to
400 Level NE Plan
page 81

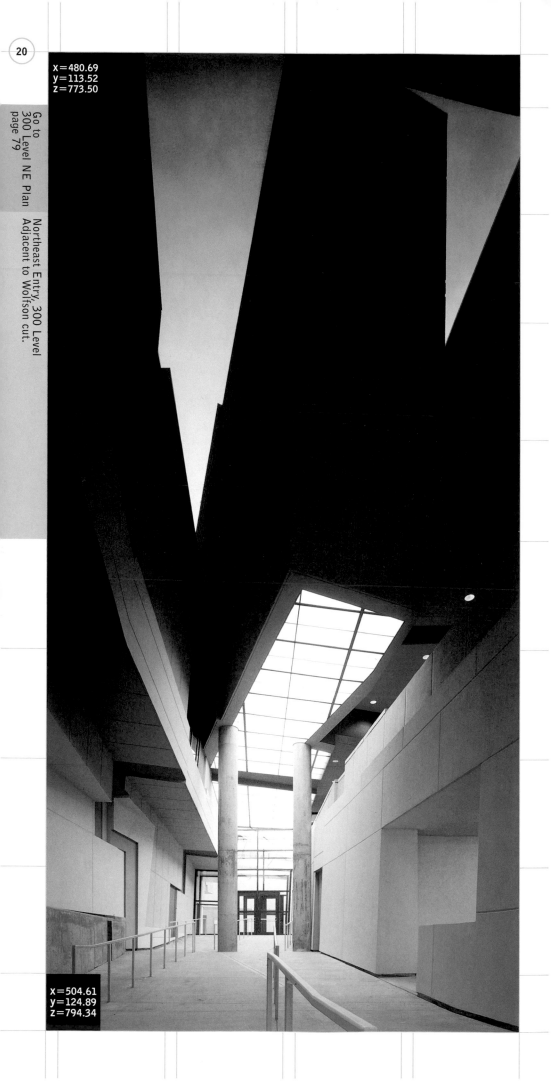

x=480.69
y=113.52
z=773.50

Go to
300 Level NE Plan
page 79

Northeast Entry, 300 Level
Adjacent to Wolfson cut.

x=504.61
y=124.89
z=794.34

THEORY AFTER BUILDING

K. Michael Hays

The autonomy of
formal construction

Contemporary architecture's situation was never more radically theorized than by Manfredo Tafuri. Historicizing architecture's intellectual project in the agonized matrix of the bourgeois metropolis (and refusing any periodization of a postmodernism), Tafuri formulates the entire cycle of modernism — preeminently including the experiments of Aldo Rossi and the neo-avant-garde of Peter Eisenman — as a unitary development in which the avant-gardes' visions of utopia come to be recognized as an idealization of capitalism, a transfiguration of the latter's rationality into the rationality of autonomous form — architecture's "Plan," its ideology. Like the blasé personality of Georg Simmel, bourgeois art and architecture essentially and contradictorily register the very forces that assure their ineffectuality. Having first been exploded by the shock and distress of the metropolis (expressionism), and then, with a sardonic detachment, taken an inventory of its surrounding remains (dadaism), bourgeois architectural thought must conclude that "the subject" itself is the only impediment to the smooth development of the fully rationalized technocratic plan that was to become the total system of capital. One had to pass from Edvard Munch's cathartic Scream to Ludwig Hilberseimer's metropolitan machine to Peter Eisenman's houses of cards — the ultimate architectural sign of self-liquidation through the autonomy of formal construction — wherein the homeostatic regulation of form becomes the ideological training ground for life in the desacralized, distracted, posthumanist world. "Among all the avant-garde movements, autonomy of formal construction no longer necessarily meant controlling daily experience through form. They were now disposed to accept the idea that it is experience that dominates the subject. The problem was to plan the disappearance of the subject, to cancel the anguish caused by the pathetic (or ridiculous) resistance of the individual to the structures of domination that close in upon him, to indicate the voluntary and docile submission to those structures of domination as the promised land of universal planning . . . ."

La poésie n'est pas que dans le verbe. Plus forte est la poésie des faits.

Le Corbusier, Vers une Architecture

Manfredo Tafuri, Architecture and Utopia (Design and Capitalist Development) (Cambridge: MIT Press, 1976), 73.

See Kipnis on "Rowe's best trick" page 171

Colin Rowe, "Introduction," in Five Architects (New York: Wittenborn, 1972), 6–7.

Gregory L. Ulmer, "The Object of Post-Criticism," in The Anti-Aesthetic: Essays on Postmodern Culture, ed. Hal Foster (Port Townsend: Bay Press, 1983); Peter Eisenman, "Post-Functionalism," Oppositions 6 (Fall, 1976).

Odd as it may seem at first, Tafuri's analysis is not incommensurate with that of contemporary architecture's other ur-theorist, Colin Rowe. For Rowe agrees that, if the historical architectural avant-garde shared common ideological roots with Marxism, it also shared a Marxian philosophical ambition to interfuse form and word — variously articulated as expression and content, system and concept, practice and theory, building and politics. That the fusion process ultimately failed entailed a shift in the terms in which the experience of modernity itself was thought: a shift from modernity, fully developed, as the essential desired achievement of architecture to modernity as architecture's limiting condition.

Feeling the force of this shift, Rowe forthrightly exposes what seems to be the only possible choice for the neo-avant-garde: adhere to the forms, the "physique-flesh" of the avant-garde, and relegate the "morale-word" to incantation. For if the latter has been reduced to "a constellation of escapist myths," the former "possess an eloquence and a flexibility which continues now to be as overwhelming as it was then." The measure of architecture no longer lies in the efficacy with which it prefigures a new and better social world, but rather in its achievement, within the contingent historical conditions of the modern, of meeting the demands of the flesh, as it were, of elevating form as its own language without reference to external sentiments, rationales, or indeed, social visions. The plastic and spatial inventions of cubism and contructivism, Giuseppe Terragni and Le Corbusier, remain the standard specific to the ideologically indifferent medium of architecture itself. But it is through acceptance of that standard and the repetition of just those simulacra that the contemporary architect aspires to be intelligible. From Rowe's position, the true potential of architecture lies not in the prospect of its popular or technological relevance, but the possibility of its autonomy.

Learning his historical-theoretical lessons from Tafuri and Rowe, Eisenman, from his early houses right up to the present, has consistently and relentlessly pursued a mode of thinking that Gregory Ulmer has called "post-criticism," which is constituted primarily by the application of certain devices of modernism to critical representations. A historically adequate architecture, according to Eisenman, should be not so much a subjective innovation as a search for objective knowledge that lies outside the artist — as potential within the very materials of architecture. Such a research discovers the new in the given, and discovers it immanently, through an articulation and redistribution of the elements of the architectural medium. Hence the importance of representation: the architectural object, in this view, is just a representation and constant exploration of architectural knowledge itself.

But as important as the cognitive vocation of this formal object-become-simulacrum of process is the implication of what is entailed when architecture represents the very process of "architecting": that the autonomy of architecture appears not because of some preordained decision to exclude other considerations but as the consequence of a felt demand of history itself. Tafuri's symptomology returns: the historical avant-garde was a premonitory aestheticization of precisely the subjective alienation and dispersion that would arrive fully geared up (or wound down to nothing) in the postwar consumer culture of America; and the search for absolute autonomy is little but a bathetic replay of the avant-garde's self-destructive project. "The return to language is a proof of failure," asserts Tafuri; but that return is not so much chosen by the architect as it is imposed by the regressive conditions of present consumer society, "bored and in need of sedatives." The "removal of form from the domain of daily experience . . . is not because of any inability of the architect, but rather because this 'center' [of discourse, of order] has been historically destroyed."

See Zaera-Polo on "architectural knowledge rather than . . . production"
page 28

Manfredo Tafuri, "L'architecture dans la Boudoir," Oppostions 3 (May, 1974), 45, 55; Manfredo Tafuri, "The Ashes of Jefferson," in The Sphere and the Labyrinth (Cambridge: MIT Press, 1987), 301.

For all the advances made in architectural theory since Tafuri and Rowe, theory has remained largely within the dialectic between the universality of autonomous form and the universality of form's historical contingency. This, in any case, was part of the background understanding I had in mind when I visited the Aronoff Center for Design and Art at the University of Cincinnati: that the struggle of architecture to rationalize itself through autonomous formal operations alerts us not to architecture's success, but to the way it comes to grief against its historical situation, which has shut down certain social and aesthetic functions that architecture previously performed. The other fact I had in mind was that the most advanced design practices, Eisenman's included, have tended to take on the categories and concepts of theory as their guides. This is surely the case in the Aronoff Center, which should be seen as a transitional work, departing from the layered grids of the "artificial excavations" and initiating the more recent experiments with computerized generation of complex form — theory becomes form almost without authorial intervention. But the Center, I soon discovered, is one of a few buildings that — perhaps despite its author's intentions — reminds us that architecture will always exceed its theorization.

For my own understanding of Eisenman's contribution to the dialectic of autonomy and historical contingency, see K. Michael Hays, "Allegory Unto Death: An Etiology of Eisenman's Repetition," in Artificial Excavations (Montreal: Canadian Centre for Architecture, 1993).

Here I should accentuate the distinction between theories like Tafuri's that construct the ideological unconscious of architecture and those like Eisenman's that seek to account for architecture's counterideological thrust with theorizations of more complex forms. Of the latter type, let us stipulate, for the sake of the point I am trying to make, that there is no better theoretical account of the counterideological form of Aronoff Center and no better prediction of its experiential effects than Sanford Kwinter's article, "The Genius of Matter," a passage from which can stand as summary: "The Cincinnati project is an architecture literally fraught with movement, waves, flow, and this guarantees the continual infolding of external influences, the continual recycling and rendering productive of chance perturbations collected in real time at the site." In an elaborate transduction of theories of complexity to architectural form, Kwinter recounts the formal systems, the this and the that, that generate the building. But what I experienced at the Center

Sanford Kwinter, "The Genius of Matter: Eisenman's Cincinnati Project," in Peter Eisenman & Frank Gehry (New York: Rizzoli International, 1991).

was not <u>this</u> or <u>that</u> but rather something that <u>started</u> <u>from</u> this and that, which is altogether different, for this and that have been displaced; and the reading protocol of Kwinter (and Eisenman) proves to be as reductive as it is accurate. And so, to the extent that a theory like Tafuri's or Kwinter's succeeds either in its uncovering the ideological imperative or in its predicting the counterideological experiential effects of a building, it also fails, since the more powerful the model constructed of either type, the less chance of any resistance or transformation or excess on the part of the architecture.

The Aronoff Center has no outside; it is all interior. What of it you "see" from the main boulevard to the north is just the hill reproducing itself in different colors; what appears to be building is just the matrix out of which the space inside is produced. The legibility of the message made available in the views of the model is completely denied the visitor to the building. What one perceives, rather, are the pulses of space and the different registers of public and private scenes that make up the "community space" — which is what Dean Jay Chatterjee calls the gap left between

See Kolbowski on "hyper-articulated spatial vignettes" page 137

the three old buildings and the new "wave"— with its platforms and terraces that step up through the main space and delineate areas for review of the studio work, a bookstore, a gallery, eating facilities, and so forth. What you perceive is space sliding away from you, doubling back behind you, below you, over you. Small tears in the space allow glimpses into more layers beyond; in one moment, from the entrance at the top of the site, one can see through a set of apertures all the way to the other entrance, 45 feet and six inches below. The "chevrons" that have been pulled in from the circulation systems of the old buildings puncture the space of the "wave." The corridors of the "wave" of studios twist and tunnel vision but never close or focus it. And it is difficult to suppress anecdotal impressions and memories (usually regarded as pretheoretical and therefore degraded). The whole reminds me of my (uneducated) experience of certain music — I am thinking of Alexander Scriabin's cabalistic, slightly mad, late piano sonatas, for example,

x=263.17
y=131.90
z=749.50

Go to 500 Level NC Plan page 86

Go to chevron page 86

See Kwinter on "the player-piano approach" page 160

where the extreme chromaticism pushes the music right up to the brink of atonality but is never systematized by the theoretical formulation of dodecaphonics — where I can enjoy not <u>what</u> the music is but <u>that</u> it is. Now it is true that in certain large rooms like the studios, the generative systems are generally legible in the encodings of gypsum wall board and paint, but such information and the materials of such messages are completely overwhelmed by <u>all the rest</u>, the surplus of space whose inadvertent effects appear without having been sought. I would characterize the space of the Aronoff Center as anticipatory space — not the logical outcome of a prior theoretical system but a space waiting for a not-yet-discovered theoretical account, which could, in turn, provide concepts for new ways of practicing space.

It is understandable, then, that, confronted with such space, theorists are led to a consideration of the field of architectural <u>affects</u> that previous critical and historical techniques have been remiss to assess. The contributions of Sanford Kwinter and Jeffrey Kipnis to this volume are examples of theory partially undoing itself in order to acknowledge what the building does differently. That Kwinter refers to the event of interpretation and Kipnis must resort to a language of madness and odor in order to outdo strictures both linguistic and architectural are, perhaps, as much symptomatic as therapeutic of the situation I am characterizing, but such misalignments of theory and building are part of an emerging project to respect that about architecture which is excessive, radically incomplete, and formless.

The Aronoff Center forces the recognition that theory must reserve for the architectural object the chance to provoke radically new responses not anticipated by a prior reading instrument that would try in vain to

I recorded these impressions before I read Sanford Kwinter's meditations on Romantic music in his article for this volume. That we both were reminded of musical analogs is symptomatic of the way the Aronoff Center conveys its punctual effects.

Freud construed <u>affect</u> to be a measure of the excitation or "emotion" that is attached to any idea. Affects are purely somatic and "instinctual" impulses that "cathect" ideas in the process of attaining expression.

account for it in advance or even describe it afterward. Now, I do not intend here to return to some older privileging of the object and its authenticity or originality (though that is one charge I would have to take seriously). Nor do I intend to help usher in some post-theoretical, neo-pragmatist period (which I regard as a mealymouthed, liberal version of the end-of-ideology thesis). Rather I wish to point to the post–Tafuri–and–Rowe phobia of a language of senti-ments that might register the desires and pleasures of things, images, and experiences, and to suggest that this be understood as a reaction formation during a latency period of architectural theory. From Tafuri's structural totalization of architecture and capitalism according to the codes of rationalization and planifi-cation to Eisenman's own anti-anthropomorphism according to the codes of nonvertabraeic form, theory has handed architecture the fig leaf of autonomy and channeled architecture's libido into historical impera-tives and counterideological resistances. However much these theories of autonomy are in advance of older forms of sublimation (historicism, functional-ism, and the like), to read architecture as an isomorph of the categories and operations of theory can be as reductive as those readings that trace architecture to an inevitable reflection of a wholly predictable tech-nological or economic context, that give no reciprocal force to architecture as a social production. In our successful theorizing of autonomy we have theorized ourselves out of the means to see architecture as exceeding our theories.

Reaction formations (like shame and disgust) and sublimations (like aesthetic and moral claims) are the two processes that Freud saw as muffling sexual impulses during the child's latency period.

See Kipnis on "pheromonal translunacy" page 177

K. Michael Hays is professor of architec-tural theory at Harvard's Graduate School of Design. He is the founding editor of Assemblage and is now working on a comprehensive history of architectural design theory from 1968 to the present.

THE MAKING OF THE MACHINE: POWERLESS CONTROL AS A CRITICAL STRATEGY

Alejandro Zaera-Polo

The construction of the Aronoff Center for Design and Art at the University of Cincinnati is an important event, not only within the overall project of its author, Peter Eisenman, but also as perhaps the most radical embodiment of one of the paradigms of a contemporary critical practice in architecture. Eisenman's career has been a continuous research on the possibilities of a contemporary critical practice, that is, a practice whose product is fundamentally architectural knowledge rather than direct architectural production. He asks the question, Is architectural knowledge possible in the age of media and the marketplace, at a time when ideologies seem to be vanishing? At a time when the critical practice of architecture is clearly divided between those embracing and those resisting the forces of the market and the media, Eisenman's position — the Aronoff Center is perhaps the most poignant example to date — is a paradigmatic alternative. Eisenman argues that a critical practice must occupy a position of resistance to the space of power, while acknowledging the zeitgeist. Those who occupy a position of resistance tend to reject the zeitgeist as an operative condition. Traditionally, those who try to construct a critical practice from within the market and the media embrace it. The niche that Eisenman identifies within the space of this debate is therefore unique, for he attempts to construct a position of resistance, perhaps of absolute resistance, without rejecting the zeitgeist as an operative space. If contemporary architects who

The sciences do not try to explain, they hardly even try to interpret, they mainly make models. By a model is meant a mathematical construct which, with the addition of certain verbal interpretations, describes observed phenomena. The justification of such a mathematical construct is solely and precisely that it is expected to work.

John Von Neumann

The Making of the Machine:
Powerless Control as a Critical Strategy
Alejandro Zaera-Polo

A formula for a
nonconservative critical resistance

claim to occupy a position of resistance operate most-
ly by finding a point of leverage to oppose the dominant forms of spatial organization — whether through
local techniques or idiosyncrasies, historical arguments, or simply self-affirmation as the origin of
countermovement — Eisenman constructs an even
more radical resistance: he defends the independence
of architecture as a discipline by discarding the points
of leverage suspected of being allied with or derived
from latent power structures. His absolute resistance
to the space of power is produced not by exerting a
subjective opposition to it but rather through the
replacement of the subject, always thought to represent some form of power, by an instrumental or
machinic process. By replacing origin, presence, and
author with arbitrariness, absence, and machinic
behavior, he has found a formula for a nonconservative critical resistance that also operates within the
space of the zeitgeist. Eisenman's major discovery is
to have located the space of a machinic performance
as a space of absolute resistance within the zeitgeist:
he has become the first truly machinic architect, not
in the sense of production but in the sense of the purely ideological. Eisenman's machines are intended to
disengage the traditional coupling between power and
control, to remain in control of the project without
becoming an instrument of the zeitgeist or of any
other power structure, and to operate within it as a
critical force. "I have been always interested in control, not in power," Eisenman says.

This revealing statement illuminates the experiments he has been
developing throughout his career.
As a radical conclusion to these
experiments, the Aronoff Center is
well worth careful examination, for
it may shed light on several
domains of contemporary architectural practice, particularly with
respect to architecture's relations
to power structures.

The Aronoff Center is neither the
tautological application of forms
based on accumulated disciplinary
knowledge nor the embodiment of
the paradigms of the zeitgeist; neither an act of opposition to the
zeitgeist nor a revolution in the

From Peter Eisenman's presentation to the Complexity Seminar at the Architectural Association, London, 1994.

"Kuhnian" sense. Rather, it is a form of knowledge more able to embrace emerging forms of production or economic integration. The Center is the result of a process engineered to generate accidental emergence and affiliations, not the outcome of a process finely tuned to meet the requirements of an emerging demand. But more important perhaps than trying to discover the specific achievements of the building, such as naming the qualities of the space and material distributions that the project generates — post-Cartesian space, supple geometry, and folds — is the fact that architecture, traditionally subjected to dominant "natural" orders — structural, functional, symbolic, linguistic — is here liberated from them without abandoning the idea of epistemological rigor and control. In the Aronoff Center, Eisenman explores the possibilities of an "artifactual" practice, a practice that moves beyond the limits established by the dominant forms of the conventional discipline. "Architecture" can only emerge once architects are able to disengage the discipline from its historical and local context and start thinking of the sequence of disciplinary operations as a purely artificial construct. To speak no longer with a language but with a metalanguage is what Eisenman calls the architecture of architecture, the practice of architecture as writing. In its stubborn compliance with its own displacing program and in its contradictions to and negotiations with the site, structure, mechanical systems, and functional requirements, the Aronoff Center is a critical manifesto on the limits of the building industry, of typological determinism, of architecture's relationship with context, and, ultimately, of the language of architecture. The building cannot be assessed by conventional terms. Rather, it must be seen as a series of fragmentary comments about the nature of architecture, which are revealed by the design and construction process, as well as within Eisenman's specific project of a critical practice.

The Aronoff Center occupies a distinctive place among the projects that constitute Eisenman's long and consistent search into the possibilities of a critical practice. The building explores techniques similar to those present since his early projects, such as the juxtaposition of multiple grids as traces of multiple parameters, which tend to penetrate the architectural object not as a figure in itself but as a structure presenting multiple relationships within different fields. However, compared with Eisenman's Checkpoint Charlie housing,

Romeo and Juliet project, or Wexner Center for the Visual Arts, the Aronoff Center does not use the tension generated between rigid, abstract, and orthogonal grids as the geometrical argument of the project. Here the grid is generated through the transformation of specific traces of the site and the program. In other projects Eisenman seemed to propose that a building is determined by its relationships to a contradictory multiplicity of grids extending beyond the specific domain of the project. What is interesting here with respect to previous or later projects and buildings is the exploration of categories specific to the most traditional definition of the discipline. The Aronoff Center is the first of a series of projects — the Greater Columbus Convention Center and the Emory Arts Center come later — in which Eisenman's work is closer to experimentation with concrete architectural parameters and, therefore, where his research comes closer to defining an architectural knowledge that moves beyond mere resonance with the forms of a political or social zeitgeist.

In the Aronoff Center there is a new formulation of Eisenman's antimodern technique to enforce coherence between the field and the object, the figure and the background. Perhaps more importantly, it is one of his first attempts to redefine the background as a figure, to initiate a dialogue of figure-figure. The most important evolution with respect to his previous projects, and especially to its closest predecessor, the Wexner Center, is the use of fields that are no longer abstract but rather are determined by objects already occupying the site. Within Eisenman's overall project, the Aronoff Center becomes the inflection point between the research developed before the Wexner Center, which was based on the tension generated between different fields, and the later phase, where accidental, singularized, coherent, but differentiated fields without relationships to external territories constitute the basis of the work. In Rebstock Park, the Max Reinhardt Haus, and the Haus Immendorf, models extracted from other disciplines, like the "Soliton Wave" and "Frederick's Transition," are grafted into the project "top-down" to generate spatial effects of a differentiated coherence, perhaps more in accordance with the zeitgeist of a scientific era. The Aronoff Center is an attempt to construct a singularized field of artificial specificity out of its contextual relationships, a "bottom-up" process performed through the

The Making of the Machine:
Powerless Control as a Critical Strategy
Alejandro Zaera-Polo

See Forster on "the
true measure of their rupture"
page 116

encoding of accidental qualities of the site/program as indexical traces. These traces are then transformed through a set of geometrical operations into the web that constitutes the building's structure. The Center is a moment of emergence in Eisenman's work. The techniques used in its construction achieve a double effect: they operate within specifically architectural parameters in a nonconventional manner; and they avoid resorting to the application of external models that, even if singular and contingent to the specific problem, imply a negotiation with the spatiality of the zeitgeist. The techniques developed in the Center prefigure the later work and coincide with the beginning of Eisenman's use of the computer as a design tool that makes available a more complex geometry than the orthogonal grid characteristic of his early work.

The generative process of the Aronoff Center begins with the selection of a number of specific elements from the site: the curves that define the northern border of the plot are adopted as an indeterminate geometric origin; the outlines of the existing buildings and the basic structure of the new building — a chevron — are taken as indexes, devoid of their function or significant content; and the spatial quanta of function (each 40'x70'x15'6") are taken as concrete, latent qualities of the site, rather than referring to abstract, insubstantial orders.

Go to functional diagram page 49

Two parallel sets of serial transformations are applied to each set of data in order to erase the potential opposition between the new and existing buildings, to generate a seamless structure between the site and the existing buildings, and to produce a heterogeneous, nonlinear spatial web. The transformations applied to the data, which registers the existing buildings, involve two types of operations: displacements and reorientations. These techniques are ones that Eisenman has used in previous projects. They are employed to erase the oppositions between the three existing but incoherent buildings: the original College building, the Alms building, and the Wolfson building. These techniques do not alter the internal structure of their organization but rather their location in space. By processing the outlines of the existing complex into a series of "idealized chevrons," the buildings are seen to suggest, in a parallel process, an alignment first to Alms and then to Wolfson. In this way Eisenman avoids establishing any kind of hierarchy

The Making of the Machine:
Powerless Control as a Critical Strategy
Alejandro Zaera-Polo

between them and the newly generated structure. The "idealization of the chevrons" previous to this operation is probably an attempt to develop a more dominant structure out of a secondary trace of the system.

A similar process is then applied to the data taken from the natural topography. This manipulation is serial rather than parallel, as if Eisenman's interest in the topography was as a landscape in which an evaluative process generates the traces of the project. It involves five operations. The first operation is to couple the curved contours of the land with the programmatic quanta of the building to erase the traditional opposition between site and program. These quanta of programmatic space are inserted along the curved line with an exponential overlap regulated by a factor 1.6, which introduces a differential system of intervals to the project that suggest a very different space from the repetitive metrics of the abstract grid that characterize Eisenman's earlier projects. A second operation applies an "asymptotic tilt" to the programmatic quanta. This is regulated by an arbitrary 1.2 factor, which again introduces a local disjunction. A third operation is a vertical stepping of the boxes with respect to the original line. This operation seeks an effect similar to the first two, which is to subvert the horizontal datum as a global order of the project and to reintroduce the sloped topography of the site. A fourth operation is the "exponential torquing" of the volumes, which distorts differentially the programmatic spaces themselves. The final transformation of the original topographic line consists in the phase shift of the line into three layers of program, introducing similar differentiating effects in the local sectional relations of the resulting grid. The use of exponential overlaps, asymptotic tilts, and phase displacements is also geared to turn a metrics of closed intervals — a "striated space" — into a vectorial smooth space with locally differentiated metrics, although regulated by a coherent law.

The "architecture of the architecture" of the Aronoff Center is formed by two parallel processes of "accidental" rather than "substantial" topographic data from the site. The data resulting from the registration of the existing buildings is manipulated through an integrative parallel process, in which the new structure is derived from the proliferation of the traces into multiple locations. The data derived from the natural

See Barry on "the original geometric phase" page 52

Go to phase shift page 52

topography and the site is processed serially into a generation that turns the original traces into a spatially differentiated grid.

A flow chart of the operations, the architecture of the architecture of the Center looks like this:

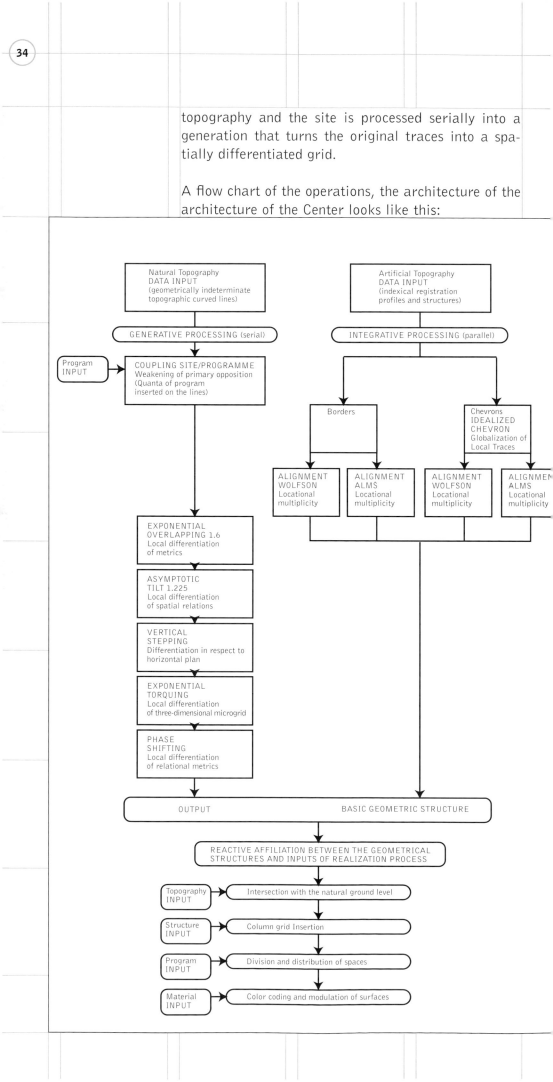

The Making of the Machine:
Powerless Control as a Critical Strategy
Alejandro Zaera-Polo

The results of these parallel processes are then juxtaposed in a graph in which unexpected local affiliations begin to emerge between the different geometries. Functional, structural, and constructive data of a more conventional nature are now deployed on the geometrical frame. This becomes the most problematic — and perhaps most revealing — stage of the process, as the geometrical frame of the building, elaborated with such sophistication, is colonized by "conventional elements of architecture": columns, doors, toilets, stairs, elevators. All previous resistance to the dominant forms of space is abandoned at the moment Eisenman's program states that the building should be performed with the most conventional technologies. The embodiment of the project is not regulated through negotiation but through contradiction with the geometrical diagram. However, the way in which these elements are usually engaged — the position of the windows with respect to the ground, the proportions of poché and usable space, the use of color with respect to the architectural elements — make one think of the multiple possibilities that architects automatically discard once they are faced with a design problem. Another interesting effect of Eisenman's machine is that the complexity of the result — which some critics have depicted as "smooth" — had to be implemented through the utmost example of "striation." All of the building trades (plumbing, tiling, painting) were carried out through a three-dimensional coordinate numerical control system implemented by an electronic laser transit on the site. Usually the implementation of the measurements on site and the layering of the trades is determined by local relationships between elements. In the Center, the constructed "smooth space" is produced from a

Unexpected local affiliations begin to emerge

Go to coordinate dimension plan page 86

global, metric organization within a system of arbitrary references. In this sense — and in the absence of any other consistent criteria of legitimation — the building is successful because it opens new alternatives to usual practices and a critique of conventional systems of architectural thought. But the most interesting aspect of Eisenman's machinic critique is that it is produced from the random encounter of arbitrary decisions and the banal conventions of social use and the construction industry.

The traditional point of view holds that the most important purpose of architecture is to produce space, not to create the possibility of architectural knowledge — or even that the possibility to produce architectural knowledge from within pure production exists. One could imagine an alternative development of the construction process of the Aronoff Center, one in which building techniques and functional requirements are not deployed on the spatial form as a contradictory argument, but rather as a more pliant matter, one that is more reactive. Looking at the juxtaposition of the concrete structure and the spatial envelope, particularly on the north elevation and the internal common space, one wonders if the choice of a cagelike steel structure internal to the enveloping surfaces — in a straightforward "balloon frame" fashion — would not have been less obtrusive spatially and would be more able to negotiate Eisenman's diagrams with the gravitational verticality. One wonders, for example, whether the major staircase could have been designed by negotiating the functional metrics with an arbitrary logarithmic order, or if the curtain wall could not have reduced the presence of the gridded metrics of production by eliminating the mullions or restraining them to one

The Making of the Machine:
Powerless Control as a Critical Strategy
Alejandro Zaera-Polo

direction. If one looks at the strategy for accommodating the air-conditioning, one can see a more
appealing result of Eisenman's machine: a "supple"
rather than contradictory negotiation of functional
requirements. As the ceiling space becomes in some
areas too constricted for the air-conditioning ducts,
the airflow regimes have to suffer violent changes in
speed and geometry; sometimes the ducts become
technically nonviable, and an alteration of the geometry of the diagram has to be made.

In making a critique of the Aronoff Center, the most
difficult problem is finding the criteria to assess the
results of a process that recognizes no origin and that
embraces arbitrariness as an operative mode.
However, in spite of the supposed arbitrariness of the
origin, as well as the development of the project purely by reaction to the relationships discovered during
the process, the building is successful in achieving its
original goals: "to blur the opposition between the
extension and the existing buildings, to accommodate
the existing topography, and to eliminate the homogeneous layering and homogeneity of the space." Finally,
one does not know whether an experiential assessment
of this building would be legitimate, as the specific
objectives of this particular project, beyond
Eisenman's overall project, seem to target some other
criteria. This could reveal some potential fractures
between Eisenman's long-term critical objectives and
his short-term practice: a global and a local Eisenman
fighting in the same building. Exploration of this tension could prove to be the most interesting aspect of
this building.

From a conversation "on-site" with Peter
Eisenman, Donna Barry, and Michael McInturf.

Alejandro Zaera-Polo
is a partner, with
Farshid Moussavi, at
Foreign Office
Architects, Ltd., in
London.

See Barry on "three-dimensional wire frame" page 57

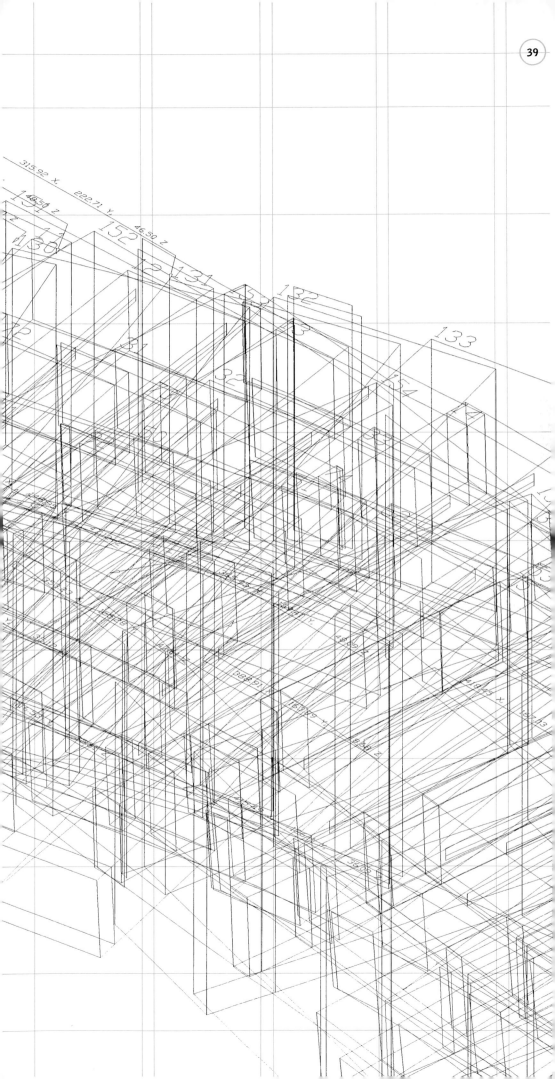

7/20/94

12/21/94

4/7/95

Construction

Go to
400 Level Entrance
page 18

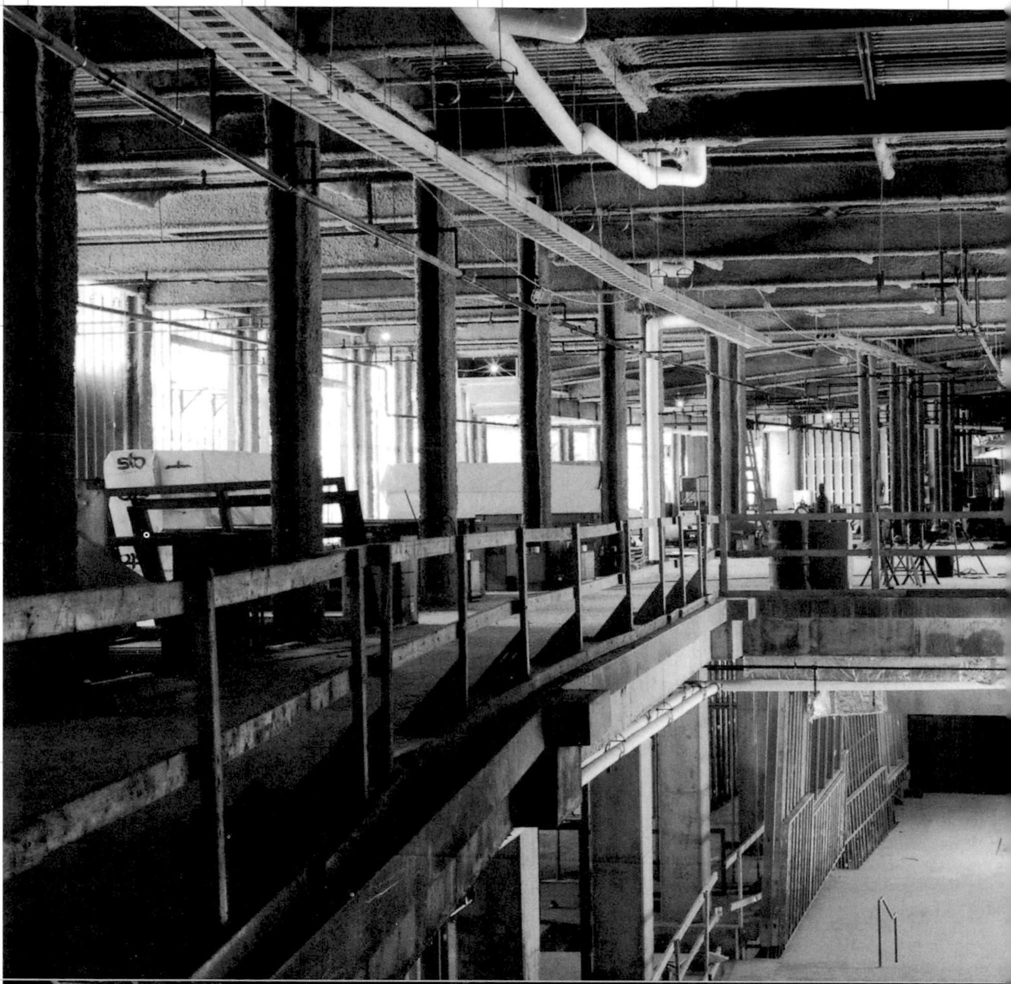

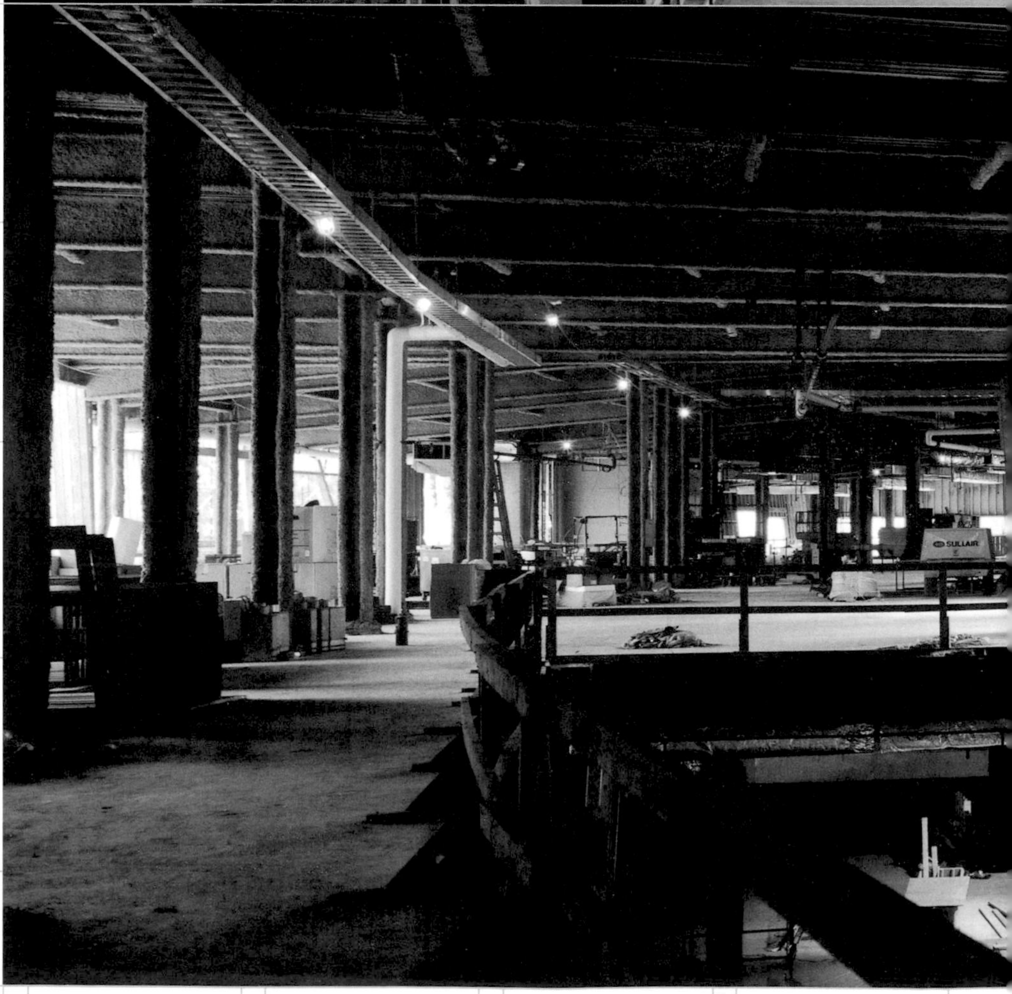
SULLAIR

Go to
500 Level NC Plan
page 87

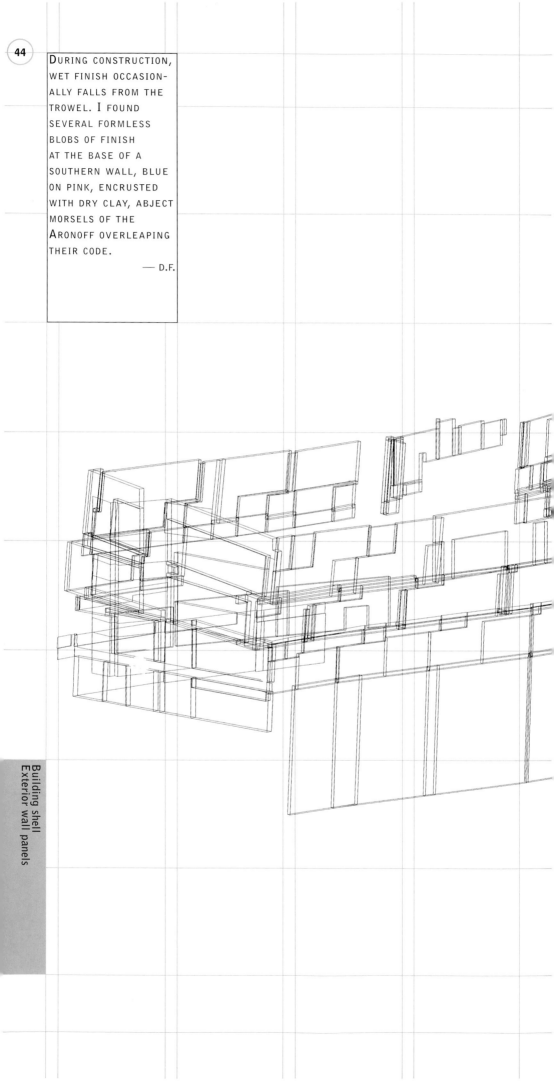

During construction, wet finish occasionally falls from the trowel. I found several formless blobs of finish at the base of a southern wall, blue on pink, encrusted with dry clay, abject morsels of the Aronoff overleaping their code.

— D.F.

Building shell
Exterior wall panels

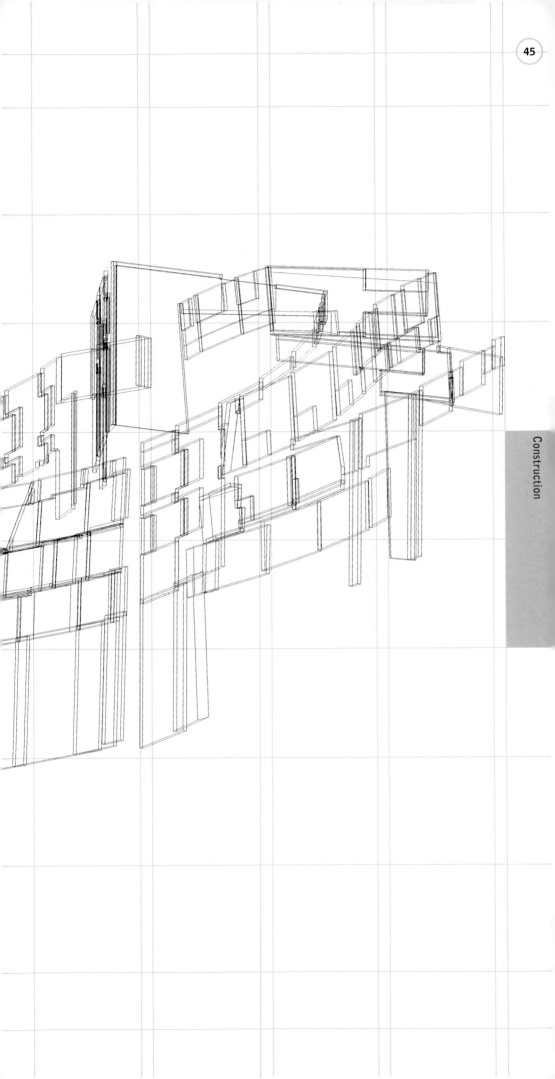

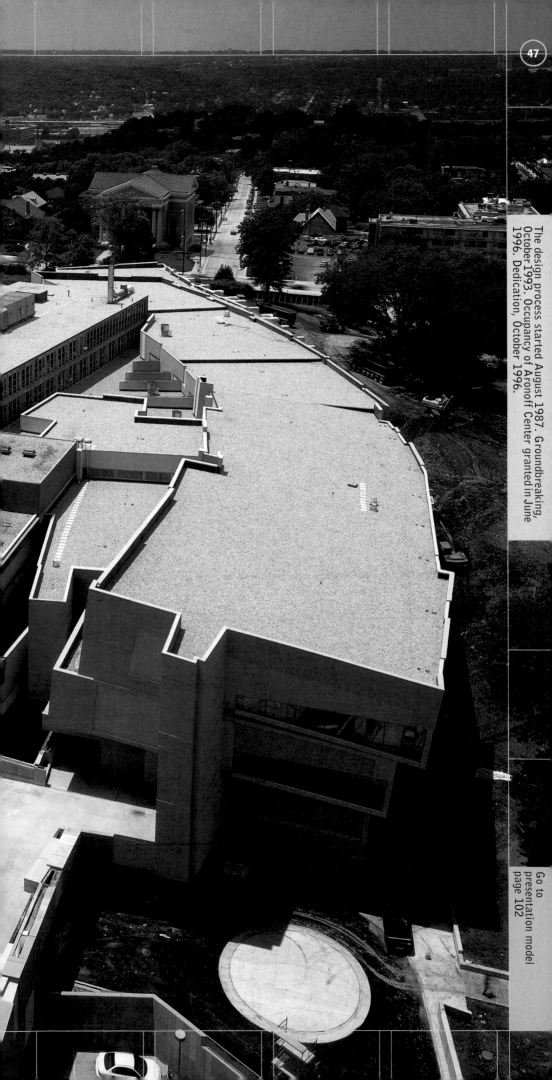

The design process started August 1987. Groundbreaking,
October 1993. Occupancy of Aronoff Center granted in June
1996. Dedication, October 1996.

Go to
presentation model
page 102

CONNECTING THE DOTS: THE DIMENSIONS OF A WIREFRAME

Donna Barry

John Barrow, Pi in the Sky (New York and Oxford: Oxford University Press, 1992), 162.

Ibid.

The space of the Aronoff Center for Design and Art challenges the conventions of both architecture and construction. Whenever a building reaches a level of complexity such as this one, the architect is compelled to invent methods and technologies with which to illustrate and build in an industry and system where "standard practice" is a dictum. At the same time, the architect cannot violate the fundamental rules of construction. The strategy for the Aronoff Center was to react to these rules while creating a space that appeared to contradict or ignore them. This strategy might be compared to "symmetry breaking." In science, the process of symmetry breaking explains observed complexity within a nonlinear system that is described mathematically by simple laws. For example, friction and air resistance must be disregarded as experimental nuisances in order to reach the essence of the science of mechanics. This reductionist view serves a limited purpose because the phenomenon of turbulence, an observed complexity, is only mathematically describable by reinserting friction and air resistance into the equation. Turbulence is motion turned irregular and can be referred to as a process of symmetry breaking that transforms the static into the dynamic. The physicist is often faced with understanding outcomes that are separated from the underlying "simple" laws of physics by a long sequence of hidden symmetry breakings, including the idea that space can be curved, that mass is not constant, and that the relative position of the body effects the measurement of the space between the object and body.

The introduction of a process similar to symmetry breaking into the design process of the Aronoff Center attempts to provide a new awareness of the human experience in space by disrupting the conventional relationships between form, function, and meaning. These relationships may not be simple and regular but complex and irregular. The challenge was how to produce the space formulated by this process. The realization of the space of the Aronoff Center was, therefore, dependent on two important developments: first, of a design process that could be analogous to symmetry breaking in science; and second, to develop a method of translation, to transform the result of this process into a descriptive form for construction.

The idea of self-similarity was considered as an example of a process analogous to symmetry breaking. Self-similarity is a process of repetition that produces an asymmetry. It implies a recursive pattern inside a pattern with a formal relation of one to the other. The difference between self-similarity and self-same recursion is that self-same recursion is necessarily symmetrical. In the case of the Aronoff Center, self-similarity sets up a duality between the original form and the copy or trace of that original form. The original and the trace are then superimposed to create a third form that incorporates them both. This notion of self-similarity is applied to the design process to produce a level of complexity that allows the distinction between the old and the new buildings to become blurred.

The realization of this building is based on a dynamic, mathematically nonlinear design process that considers real and complex systems that are not idealized through simplification. The space that resulted from the processes elaborated here begins to allow for the rediscovery of the human body as subject and object through a series of displacements that attempt to redefine the human experience in space.

Functional Diagram - Segmented line

A series of three-dimensional rectangles, which provided the basis for what came to be known as "box geometry," were placed side to side to form a segmented line. These boxes were dimensioned in plan by a functional diagram determined by the juxtaposition of studio, corridor, and office (40'0" x 70'0"). The height of a box was determined by a floor-to-floor height of 15'6" which permitted an intermediate floor-to-floor dimension. The functions were incorporated within the concept of the initial diagram so that changes in the diagram could be seen as the result of a formal intention. For example, at any one moment, the diagram might be deployed in ten alternative ways. Perhaps five of these ways could be seen as accommodating function and five not. But, perhaps only two of these ten could be seen to accommodate function while obliterating the fact that function was being simultaneously accommodated.

Go to
site model
page 102

Contextual Response

The line was transformed into a curved line to contrast with the hard rectilinear edge of the three

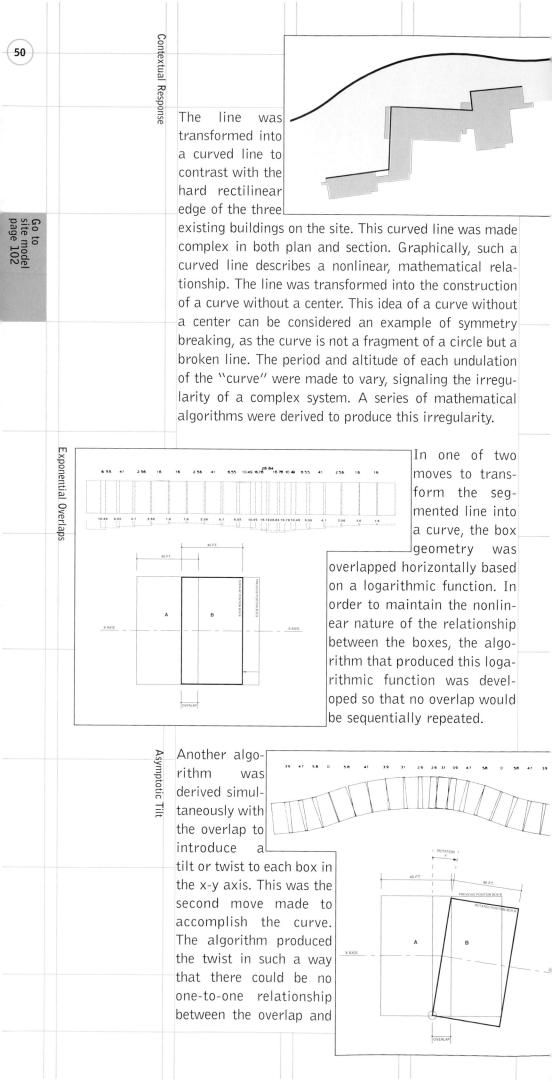

existing buildings on the site. This curved line was made complex in both plan and section. Graphically, such a curved line describes a nonlinear, mathematical relationship. The line was transformed into the construction of a curve without a center. This idea of a curve without a center can be considered an example of symmetry breaking, as the curve is not a fragment of a circle but a broken line. The period and altitude of each undulation of the "curve" were made to vary, signaling the irregularity of a complex system. A series of mathematical algorithms were derived to produce this irregularity.

Exponential Overlaps

In one of two moves to transform the segmented line into a curve, the box geometry was overlapped horizontally based on a logarithmic function. In order to maintain the nonlinear nature of the relationship between the boxes, the algorithm that produced this logarithmic function was developed so that no overlap would be sequentially repeated.

Asymptotic Tilt

Another algorithm was derived simultaneously with the overlap to introduce a tilt or twist to each box in the x-y axis. This was the second move made to accomplish the curve. The algorithm produced the twist in such a way that there could be no one-to-one relationship between the overlap and the amount of twist applied to a particular box. In other words, the exponent and phase of the plan tilts do not correspond to the exponent and phase of the overlaps, thus the asymptotic curve is generated out of the two systems. This lack of a reciprocal relationship between the two systems reinforced the idea that nothing in the lines is constant or predictable. Each condition is unique, but each move produced a describable condition. The resulting conditions are neither regular nor random; nor are they an example of individual expressionism or related to any historical iconography; they are merely an index to be marked in space.

Exponential Torque

Two moves to transform the segmented line

In order to locate the diagram in section, a relationship between the box and the floor slab had to be determined, both as a practical response to the reality of construction, as well as to the maintenance of the overriding formal logic in section. The dimension of this relationship was required to be 3'6", measured from the north bottom edge of the box along the z axis. This dimension became standard and regularized within an overall system that is irregular. To provide the same displacement of the curve in the third dimension, each box was torqued independently along the z axis, while changing direction along the x-y axis. The segmented line is torqued up at its northwest and southeast edges with a transitional flattening of torques in the middle. The torque was applied at the intersection of the floor slab and the north edge of each box. This location provided a relationship between the horizontal datum and the torqued box, allowing a consistent reading between the two elements. This set of overlapped, twisted, and torqued boxes is referred to as a _phase_. A phase contains, as it were, a snapshot of each different aspect of the curve, at any location along the line, which is continuous and irregular in three dimensions. In physics, phase transitions refer to the behavior of matter near the point where it changes from one state into another, from liquid to gas or from magnetized to unmagnetized. As singular boundaries between two realms of existence, phase transitions tend to be mathematically nonlinear. The phase of this project then also represents this nonlinear boundary between two realms of existence: between diagram/drawing and drawing/construction.

A: Phase Shift Plan

B: Phase Shift Section

The original geometric phase is shifted twice along the x axis in order to produce a series of three phases, one for each functional level (levels 400, 500, and 600). Each phase maintains the form of the original x-y twist (figure A). The applied torque to each box of each phase, however, varies at each level, so that there is no one-to-one relationship possible in section (figure B). The uppermost 600 level has the most extreme torque, while the lower 400 level has the least torque. This series of phases is descriptively referred to as the torqued solid series.

A: Torqued Solid / Torqued Trace Series, Plan

B: Torqued Solid / Torqued Trace Series, Section

The torqued solid series is shifted and copied along the x-y axis (figure A) and dropped in elevation (figure B) as a complete series. This lowering in the z plane purposely blurs the section while the shift in the y plane blurs the plan. This series of phases traced over the torqued solid series is referred to as the torqued trace series. The original phase is copied to form a self-similar series. This series is then copied to form a self-similar trace. These two series created an overlapped figure that programmatically became the "atrium space" of the building.

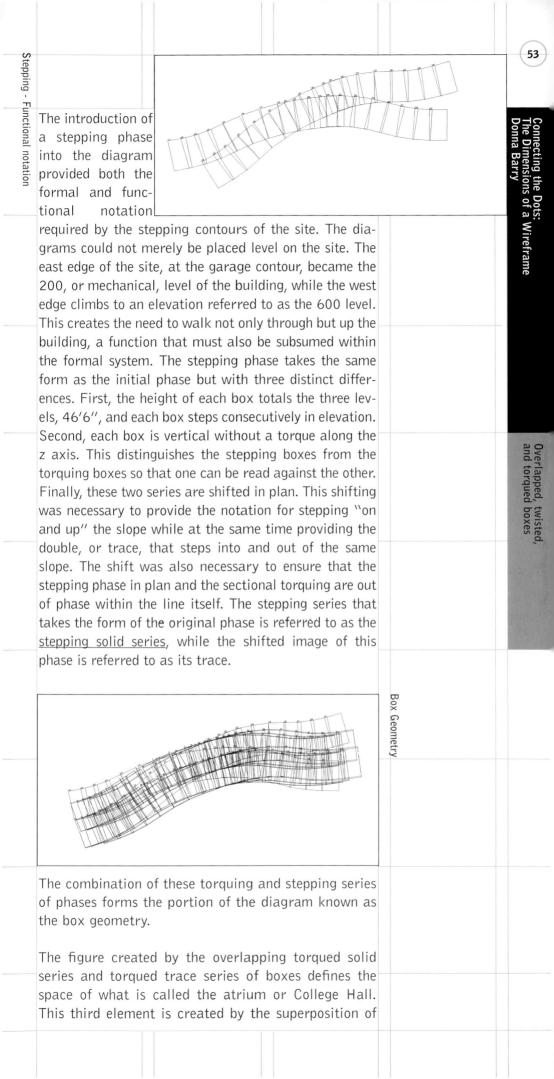

The introduction of a stepping phase into the diagram provided both the formal and functional notation required by the stepping contours of the site. The diagrams could not merely be placed level on the site. The east edge of the site, at the garage contour, became the 200, or mechanical, level of the building, while the west edge climbs to an elevation referred to as the 600 level. This creates the need to walk not only through but up the building, a function that must also be subsumed within the formal system. The stepping phase takes the same form as the initial phase but with three distinct differences. First, the height of each box totals the three levels, 46'6", and each box steps consecutively in elevation. Second, each box is vertical without a torque along the z axis. This distinguishes the stepping boxes from the torquing boxes so that one can be read against the other. Finally, these two series are shifted in plan. This shifting was necessary to provide the notation for stepping "on and up" the slope while at the same time providing the double, or trace, that steps into and out of the same slope. The shift was also necessary to ensure that the stepping phase in plan and the sectional torquing are out of phase within the line itself. The stepping series that takes the form of the original phase is referred to as the <u>stepping solid series</u>, while the shifted image of this phase is referred to as its trace.

The combination of these torquing and stepping series of phases forms the portion of the diagram known as the box geometry.

The figure created by the overlapping torqued solid series and torqued trace series of boxes defines the space of what is called the atrium or College Hall. This third element is created by the superposition of

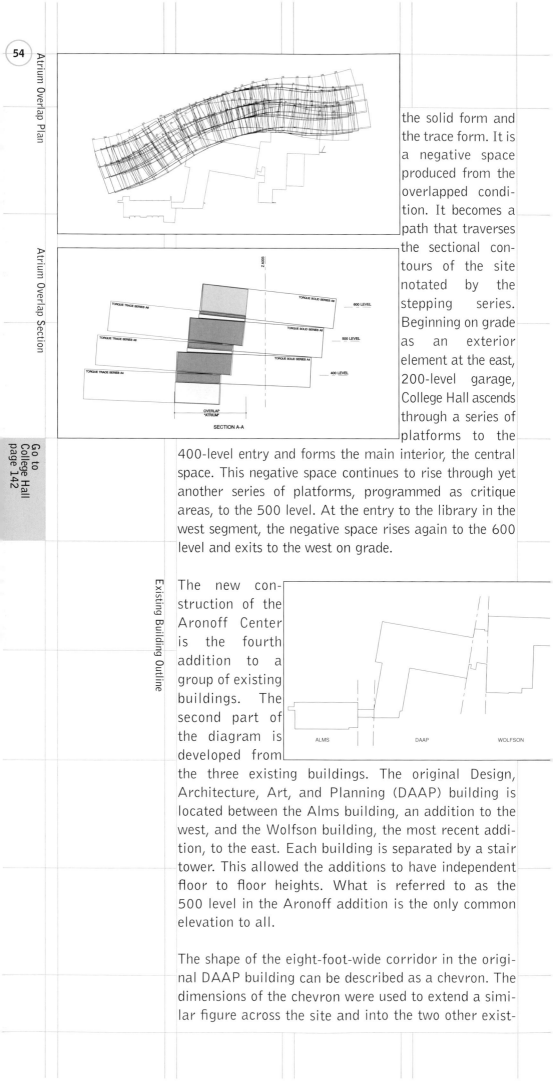

Go to
College Hall
page 142

the solid form and the trace form. It is a negative space produced from the overlapped condition. It becomes a path that traverses the sectional contours of the site notated by the stepping series. Beginning on grade as an exterior element at the east, 200-level garage, College Hall ascends through a series of platforms to the 400-level entry and forms the main interior, the central space. This negative space continues to rise through yet another series of platforms, programmed as critique areas, to the 500 level. At the entry to the library in the west segment, the negative space rises again to the 600 level and exits to the west on grade.

The new construction of the Aronoff Center is the fourth addition to a group of existing buildings. The second part of the diagram is developed from the three existing buildings. The original Design, Architecture, Art, and Planning (DAAP) building is located between the Alms building, an addition to the west, and the Wolfson building, the most recent addition, to the east. Each building is separated by a stair tower. This allowed the additions to have independent floor to floor heights. What is referred to as the 500 level in the Aronoff addition is the only common elevation to all.

The shape of the eight-foot-wide corridor in the original DAAP building can be described as a chevron. The dimensions of the chevron were used to extend a similar figure across the site and into the two other exist-

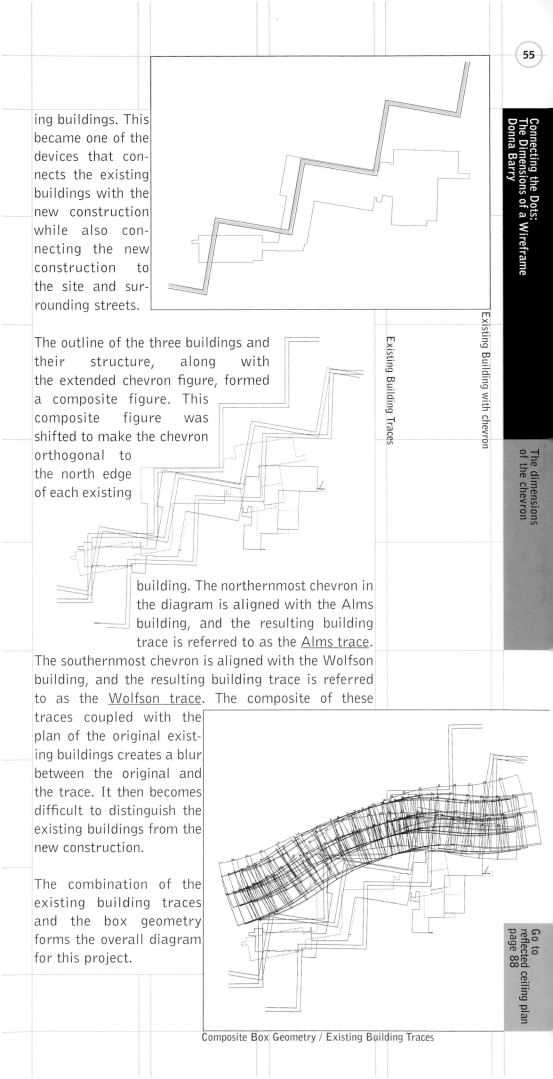

ing buildings. This became one of the devices that connects the existing buildings with the new construction while also connecting the new construction to the site and surrounding streets.

Existing Building with chevron

The outline of the three buildings and their structure, along with the extended chevron figure, formed a composite figure. This composite figure was shifted to make the chevron orthogonal to the north edge of each existing

Existing Building Traces

building. The northernmost chevron in the diagram is aligned with the Alms building, and the resulting building trace is referred to as the Alms trace. The southernmost chevron is aligned with the Wolfson building, and the resulting building trace is referred to as the Wolfson trace. The composite of these traces coupled with the plan of the original existing buildings creates a blur between the original and the trace. It then becomes difficult to distinguish the existing buildings from the new construction.

The combination of the existing building traces and the box geometry forms the overall diagram for this project.

Go to
reflected ceiling plan
page 88

Composite Box Geometry / Existing Building Traces

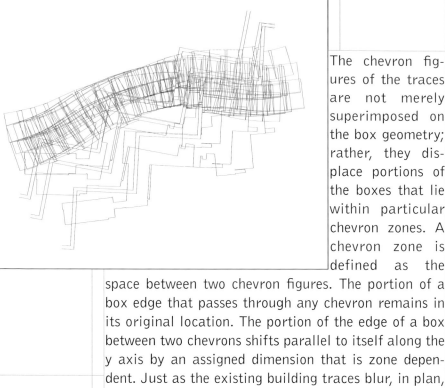

The chevron figures of the traces are not merely superimposed on the box geometry; rather, they displace portions of the boxes that lie within particular chevron zones. A chevron zone is defined as the space between two chevron figures. The portion of a box edge that passes through any chevron remains in its original location. The portion of the edge of a box between two chevrons shifts parallel to itself along the y axis by an assigned dimension that is zone dependent. Just as the existing building traces blur, in plan, the edges of the existing building, the chevron figures blur the edges of the box geometry.

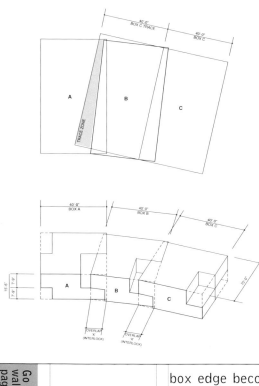

The boxes of each phase are connected at the overlap. This connection can be seen as an <u>interlock</u> (figure B). The interlock is consistently defined at the midpoint of the higher elevation box. It is reminiscent of the interlocking design of a bicycle chain. Unlike the bicycle chain, however, the interlock of the boxes cannot move; movement can only be implied through their articulation. In order to blur the interlock while at the same time providing this articulation, each box edge, (for example, Box C in diagram), is extended at the interlock by its width, 40'0" parallel to itself. This line is marked on the floor and ceiling of the box that it intersects (figure A). The area between this line and the intersecting box edge becomes recessed within the box, revealing itself as a trace. The leading edge of a trace is produced by an overlapping of the previous box edge, which obscures the interlock while creating the illusion of movement. This combination of interlocking boxes and traces is reminiscent of the moving facets of a baggage carousel or the exposed skin beneath the armor of an armadillo.

Go to
wall section
page 122

A: Interlocking within a phase

B: Interlocking section

17

Interlocking between phases: Gaskets

In the transverse section, the boxes are joined by an extension. This connection of boxes in section can be seen as an articulation or as a gasket. The gaskets are necessary to provide a continuous wall section. These box edges and gaskets are assigned a thickness of 1'2", based on the necessary material to construct the wall section.

STRUCTURAL GRID

The structural "grid" is organized by the 500-level torqued solid phase of boxes. As a result, the rectilinear column grid moves through the space independent of the form of that space. Columns pass in, out, and through the walls. Vertical on one side and sloped with the profile of the building's geometry on the other, these columns are read against the round columns that are a part of the trace of the existing building. In an attempt to integrate structural members into the box geometry, the structure itself is also obscured by aspects of the diagram. For example, not all columns are necessarily structural. In some cases they are part of a figure traced from the existing building and not related to their structuring function. This contradicts the conventional notion of the structural column. When read as a conceptual mark and not as a functional integer, the column questions the idea of the naturalness of a "column" within architecture.

The examination of space in the third dimension afforded by the computer creates a problem for construction that is based on the convention of planar extrusion. The programming and planning of functions for the Aronoff Center were organized, and a form evolved from <u>within</u> the three-dimensional wire frame provided by the computer. The space of the building was not conceived a priori, but rather emerged from the process of design. The conventional building sec-

A chevron zone and a box edge

Go to columns page 181

Go to wire frame page 38

tion is incapable of providing the information required to build this form, in part because it is not possible to cut a meaningful section through the building. Any traditional section that could be cut and drawn would be orthogonal to only one box in the wire frame.

The coordinate system typically used in surveying was thus introduced as a method for dimensioning this project. Conventional string dimensions on the floor plans were not useful to locate each box edge in reference to the column grid, and Euclidean measurements of length, depth, and thickness, relevant only in two-dimensional representations of an object 90 degrees to the picture plane, failed to capture the condition of the irregular forms. Ideas of longitude, latitude, and altitude were better suited for the twisted and torqued box geometry of this project. A bench mark was located at the northwest exterior corner of the Alms building. The edge of each box was located in relation to this control mark via x-y-z coordinate points. Coordinate points were assigned at the intersection of the floor slab and the interlocked edges of the torqued walls. A coordinate dimension plan follows each floor plan in the construction document set.

Go to
coordinate dimension plan
page 90

The ceiling plans were also documented with a coordinate dimension plan. Each room was provided with three x-y-z coordinate points defining the plane of the ceiling. These coordinate plans became a dense web of overlays. Each coordinate point is numbered and staked. This created another set of control drawings that provided a mapping of the x-y-z coordinate points of the drawings onto the actual staked points in the field. The contractors used a laser transit method of triangulation to locate points on lines and to calculate distances between coordinate points. The staked points were connected by lasers to lay out the track for the stud walls and ceilings. The numbering system of the staking plan and the staked points are not connected consecutively to create the layout of the walls. The coordinate plans are like "connect the dot drawings" without numbers. The contractor is able to "connect these dots" without the prior knowledge of the object to be drawn.

Ultimately, the conceptual transformations and the construction drawings do not describe the space of the building. The drawings cannot begin to describe the constructed space nor convey its effect on the building's users; they can only depict the form, of which the oneric space is a result. On the surfaces that define this space there are no materials that provide a scale relative to the body, since the variations in the material surfaces are indexical marks to a design system, rather than an iconic scale to the body. The building is not an expressionist form; there is clearly a logical system that has determined these surfaces and marks. But the logic remains elusive. This intrinsic logic is not intended to be easily read by the building's viewer or user. The unity of the eye/mind/body relationship typically used in understanding building and form is purposefully displaced in each move of the design process. The body itself as a vertical reference mediated by gravity is displaced by a space that activates it on a visceral level; in this sense, the only reference of scale and balance provided for the body is the body itself.

The space of this project has a labyrinthine quality. It is experienced as a logical but not easily readable path: a discovered path. One wanders and wonders . . . connecting the dots . . .

See Cobb on
"the construction of an idea"
page 97

Donna Barry worked at Eisenman Architects as a project architect on the Aronoff Center. She now teaches at Arizona State University and practices architecture in Phoenix.

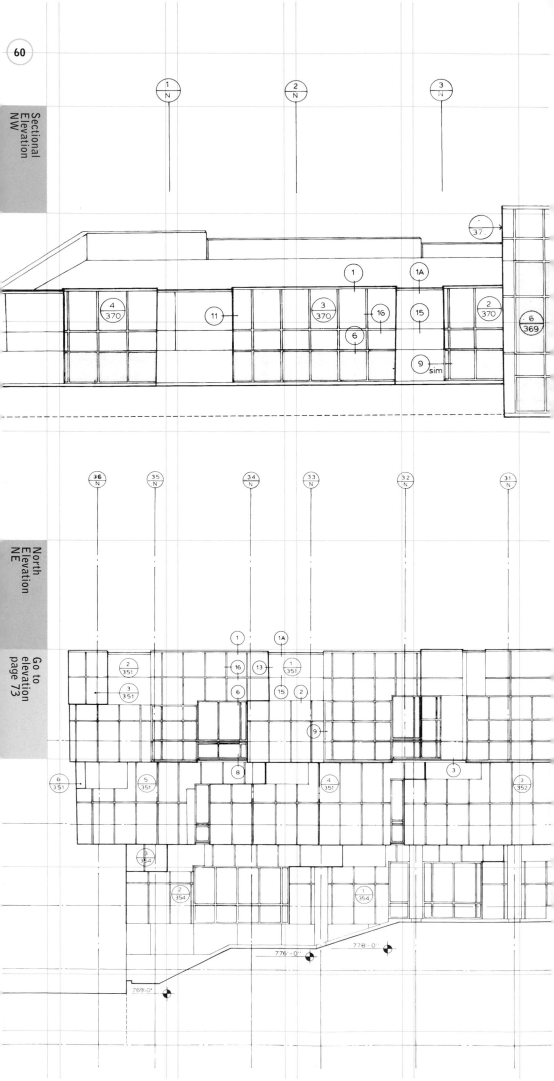

North
Elevation
NE

Go to
elevation
page 73

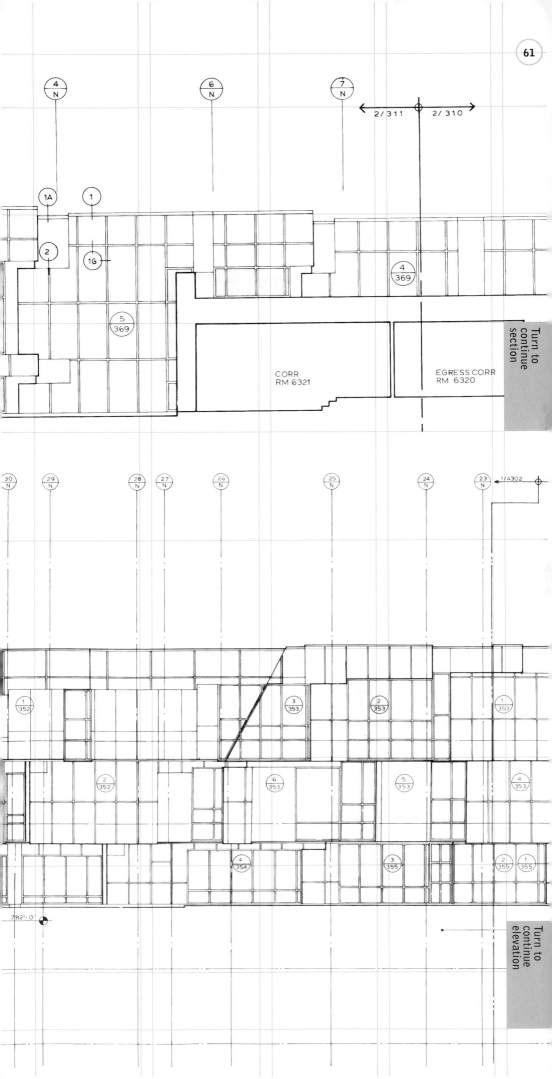

2/311   2/310

CORR
RM 6321

EGRESS CORR
RM 6320

Turn to continue section

1/A302

782'-0"

Turn to continue elevation

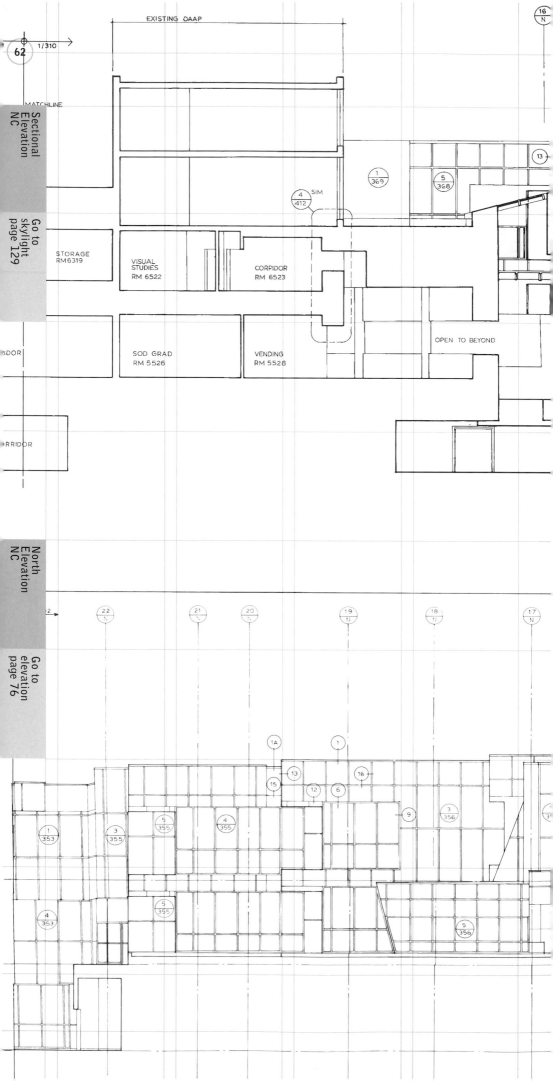

Go to
skylight
page 129

STORAGE
RM 6319

VISUAL
STUDIES
RM 6522

CORRIDOR
RM 6523

1
369

5
368

13

4   SIM
412

RRIDOR

SOD GRAD
RM 5526

VENDING
RM 5528

OPEN TO BEYOND

RRIDOR

Go to
elevation
page 76

22
N

21
N

20
N

19
N

18
N

17
N

1A

1

13

16

15

12   6

1
353

3
355

5
355

4
355

9

3
356

3

4
353

5
355

5
356

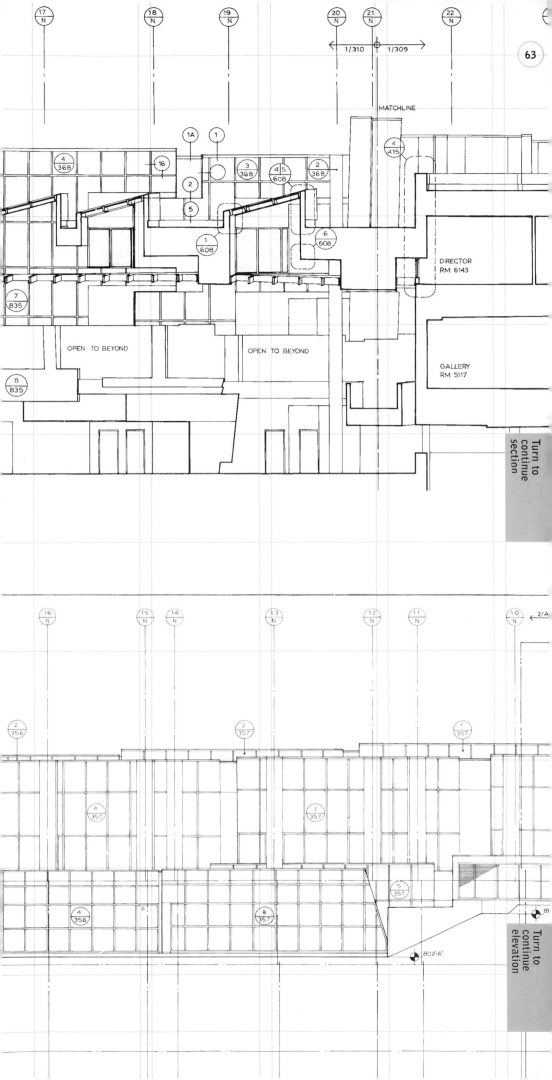

MATCHLINE

DIRECTOR
RM 6143

GALLERY
RM 5117

OPEN TO BEYOND

OPEN TO BEYOND

1/310   1/309

Turn to continue section

Turn to continue elevation

802'-6"

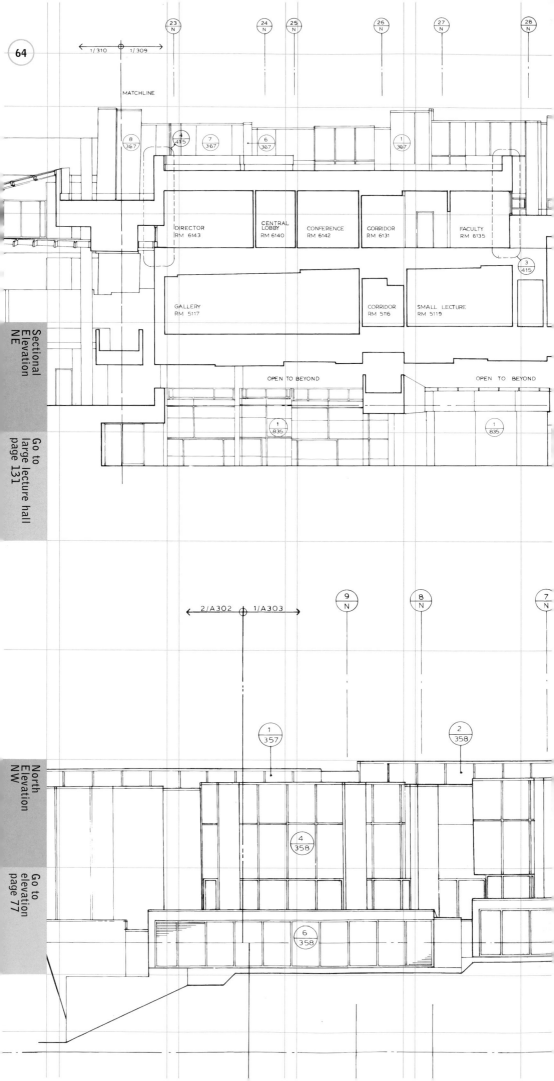

MATCHLINE

1/310   1/309

23 N   24 N   25 N   26 N   27 N   28 N

8 / 367   4 / 415   7 / 367   6 / 367   1 / 367

DIRECTOR
RM 6143

CENTRAL
LOBBY
RM 6140

CONFERENCE
RM 6142

CORRIDOR
RM 6131

FACULTY
RM 6135

3 / 415

GALLERY
RM 5117

CORRIDOR
RM 5116

SMALL LECTURE
RM 5119

OPEN TO BEYOND   OPEN TO BEYOND

1 / 835   1 / 835

Sectional
Elevation
NE

Go to
large lecture hall
page 131

2/A302   1/A303

9 N   8 N   7 N

1 / 357   2 / 358

4 / 358

6 / 358

North
Elevation
NW

Go to
elevation
page 77

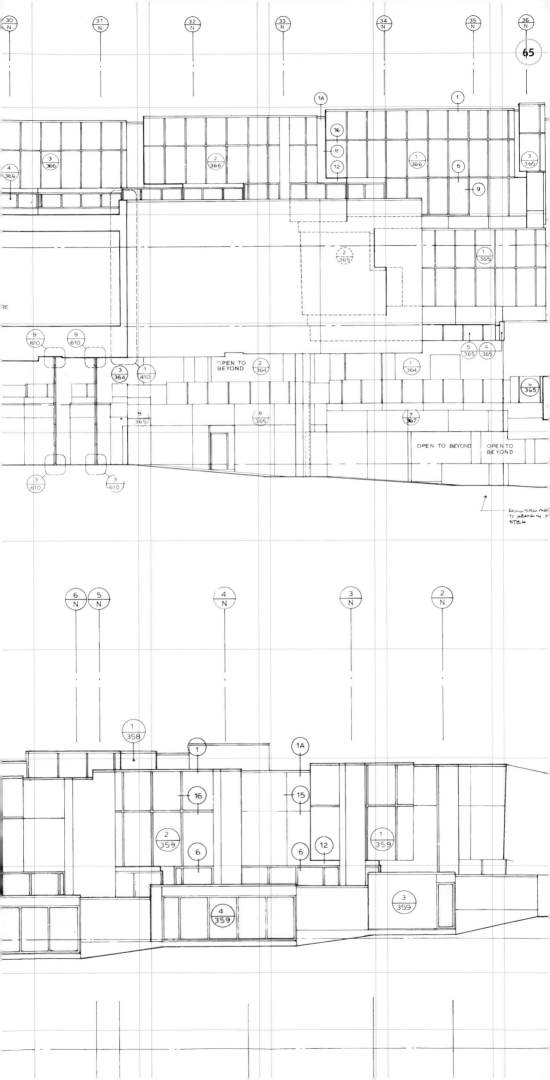

x=529.28
y=131.71
z=773.50

Go to
300 Level NE Plan
page 79

The Aronoff Center is on the University's West Campus, near the intersection of Clifton Avenue and Martin Luther King Jr. Drive.

Go to
300 Level NE Plan
page 79

x=529.97
y=153.59
z=773.56

THE BUILDING HAS NINE SPECTRAL HUES — PINK (OR SALMON), GRAY, BLUE, GREEN, WHITE, PLUS VARYING INTENSITIES OF THESE. EACH IS ASSOCIATED WITH A SPECIFIC COMPOSITIONAL OPERATION. UNCODED COLORS INCLUDE EXPOSED CONCRETE AND STAIN — WATER, RUST, MILDEW, MUD, EFFLORESCENCE, GRAFFITI — THE VARIEGATIONS OF WEATHER, ACCIDENTS, FOLLY, AND VANDALISM. ALL CONSTRUCTIONS SUFFER CHANCE MODIFICATION, BUT HERE STAIN BECOMES A SPECIES OF MATTER ALLIED TO THE ARONOFF'S COMPOSITIONAL THEORY. THIS ELEVENTH "COLOR" SERVES AS A SORT OF SHADOWLESS GNOMON THAT STEADILY PULLS THE CONSTRUCTION TOWARD THE INSTABILITIES OF DURATION, FASTER THAN GEOLOGY, SLOWER THAN THE SEDIMENTATIONS OF MEMORY.

— D.F.

Go to
400 Level NE Plan
page 81

x=550.26
y=178.18
z=801.00

x=438.76
y=118.53
z=773.50

Go to
300 Level NE Plan
page 79

x=532.18
y=223.28
z=801.00

Go to
500 Level Reflected Ceiling Plan
page 85

Exterior

x=509.48
y=224.60
z=798.92

Go to
400 Level NE Reflected Ceiling Plan
page 83

Exterior

Go to
400 Level NE Plan
page 81

x=492.24
y=219.74
z=781.17

x=323.77
y=225.41
z=801.00

Go to
500 Level NC Plan
page 87

Exterior

Go to
500 Level NC Plan
page 86

x=222.89
y=186.47
z=801.00

THE BUILDING GIVES THE SUN, AS IF IT WERE A DRAFTSMAN, A FAIRLY SMALL TASK. IT ASSIGNS THE SUN TO CONTRIBUTE SHADOWS TO THE COMPOSITION AND PARTICIPATE IN ITS DOUBLINGS AND MULTIPLICATIONS, ON THE INSTRUCTIONS OF THE ARCHITECT. THE SUN IS NOT ASKED TO REVEAL SURFACE EFFECTS, NOR TO ILLUMINATE THE BUILDING'S NINE UNNATURAL COLORS; THIS IS REALLY A JOB FOR ELECTRICITY. THESE COLORS ARE NONE OF THE SUN'S BUSINESS.
— D.F.

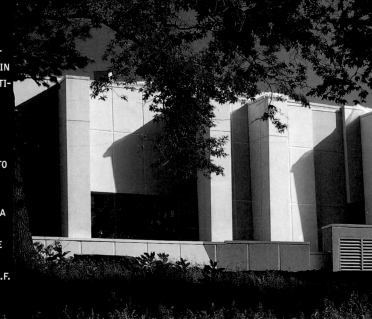

Exterior

Go to
500 Level NC Plan
page 86

x—170.79
y=166.85
z=801.00

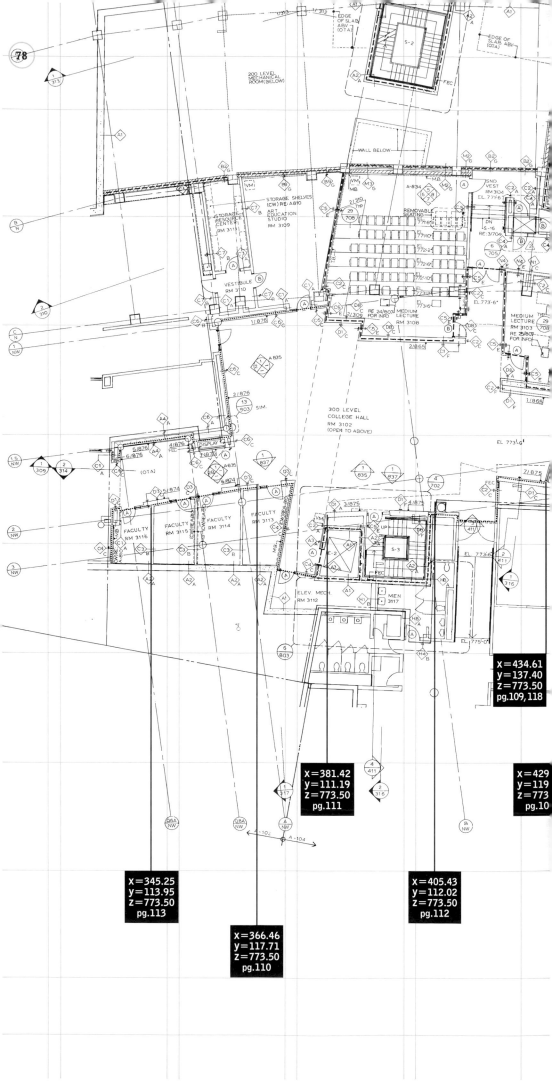

x=434.61
y=137.40
z=773.50
pg.109, 118

x=381.42
y=111.19
z=773.50
pg.111

x=429
y=119
z=773
pg.10

x=345.25
y=113.95
z=773.50
pg.113

x=405.43
y=112.02
z=773.50
pg.112

x=366.46
y=117.71
z=773.50
pg.110

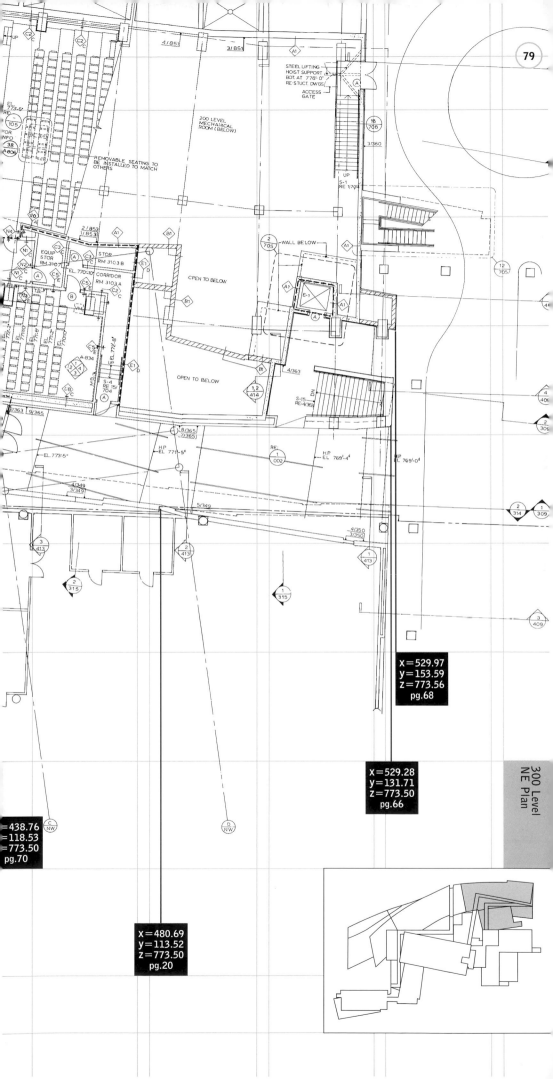

x=529.97
y=153.59
z=773.56
pg.68

x=529.28
y=131.71
z=773.50
pg.66

=438.76
=118.53
=773.50
pg.70

x=480.69
y=113.52
z=773.50
pg.20

300 Level
NE Plan

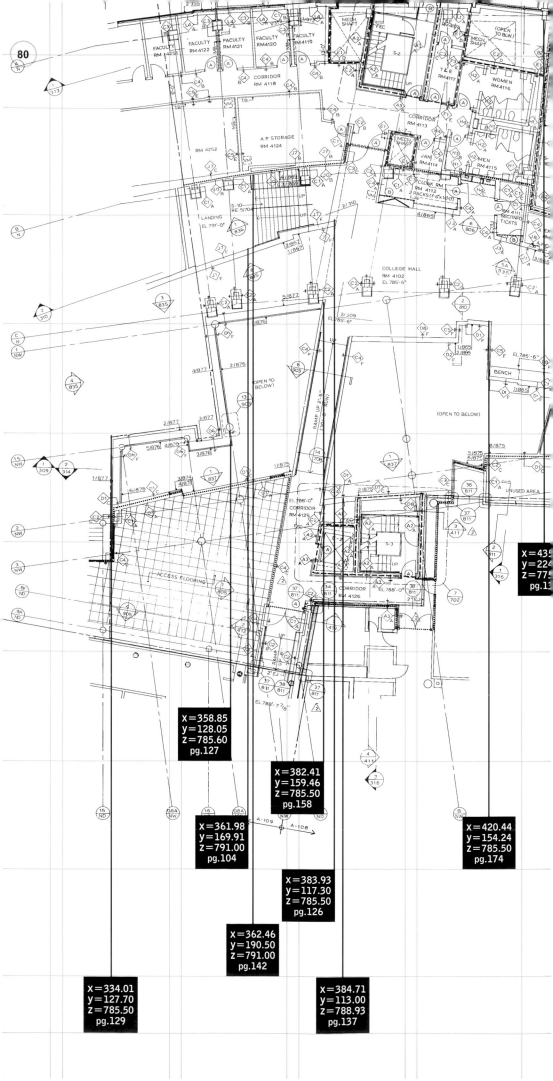

x=435
y=224
z=775
pg.13

x=358.85
y=128.05
z=785.60
pg.127

x=382.41
y=159.46
z=785.50
pg.158

x=361.98
y=169.91
z=791.00
pg.104

x=420.44
y=154.24
z=785.50
pg.174

x=383.93
y=117.30
z=785.50
pg.126

x=362.46
y=190.50
z=791.00
pg.142

x=334.01
y=127.70
z=785.50
pg.129

x=384.71
y=113.00
z=788.93
pg.137

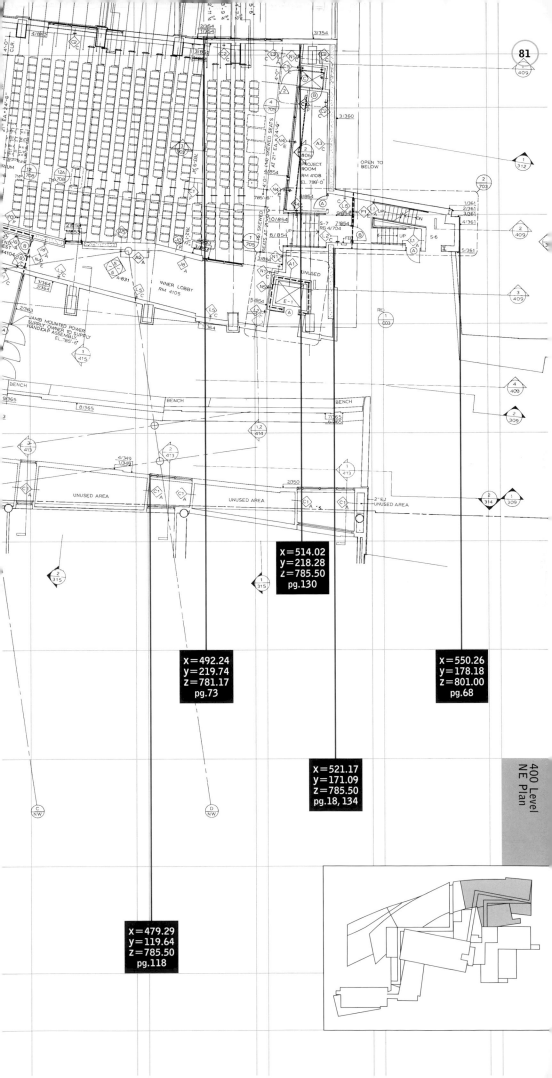

x=514.02
y=218.28
z=785.50
pg.130

x=492.24
y=219.74
z=781.17
pg.73

x=550.26
y=178.18
z=801.00
pg.68

x=521.17
y=171.09
z=785.50
pg.18, 134

x=479.29
y=119.64
z=785.50
pg.118

400 Level
NE Plan

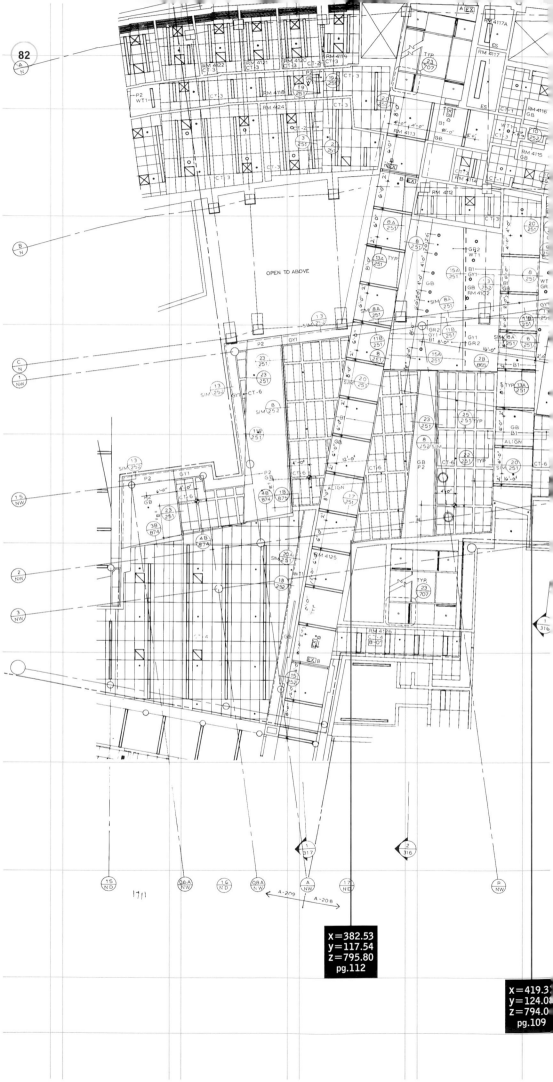

OPEN TO ABOVE

x=382.53
y=117.54
z=795.80
pg.112

x=419.31
y=124.08
z=794.0
pg.109

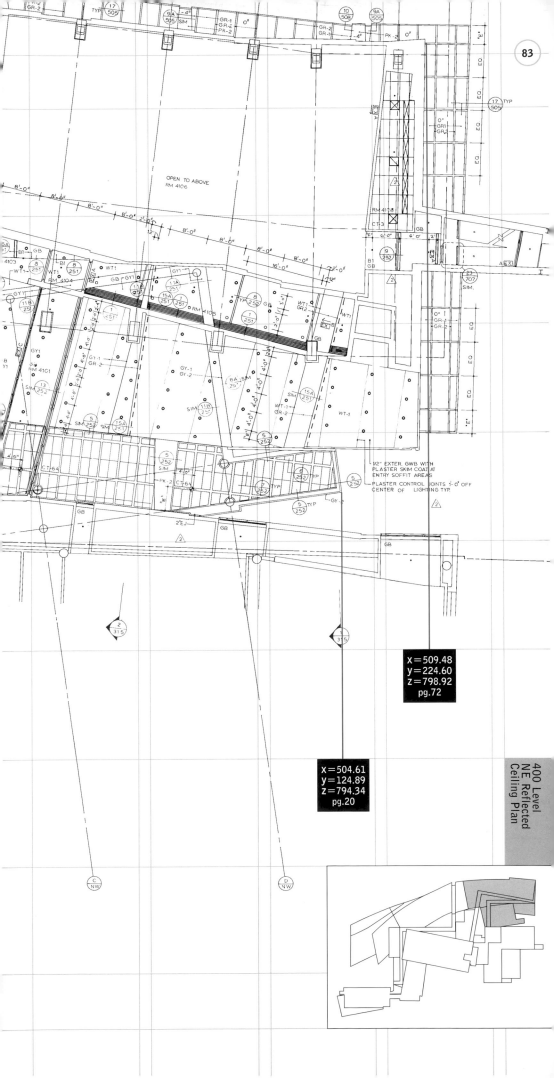

OPEN TO ABOVE
RM 410.6

RM 411.8
CT-3

1/2" EXTER. GWB WITH
PLASTER SKIM COAT AT
ENTRY SOFFIT AREAS
PLASTER CONTROL JOINTS 1'-0" OFF
CENTER OF LIGHTING TYP.

x=509.48
y=224.60
z=798.92
pg.72

x=504.61
y=124.89
z=794.34
pg.20

400 Level
N.E. Reflected
Ceiling Plan

x=378.59
y=234.38
z=812.73
pg.171

x=389.36
y=157.77
z=813.63
pg.182

x=420.18
y=152.70
z=813.02
pg.131

x=532.18
y=223.28
z=801.00
pg.71

500 Level
NE Reflected
Ceiling Plan

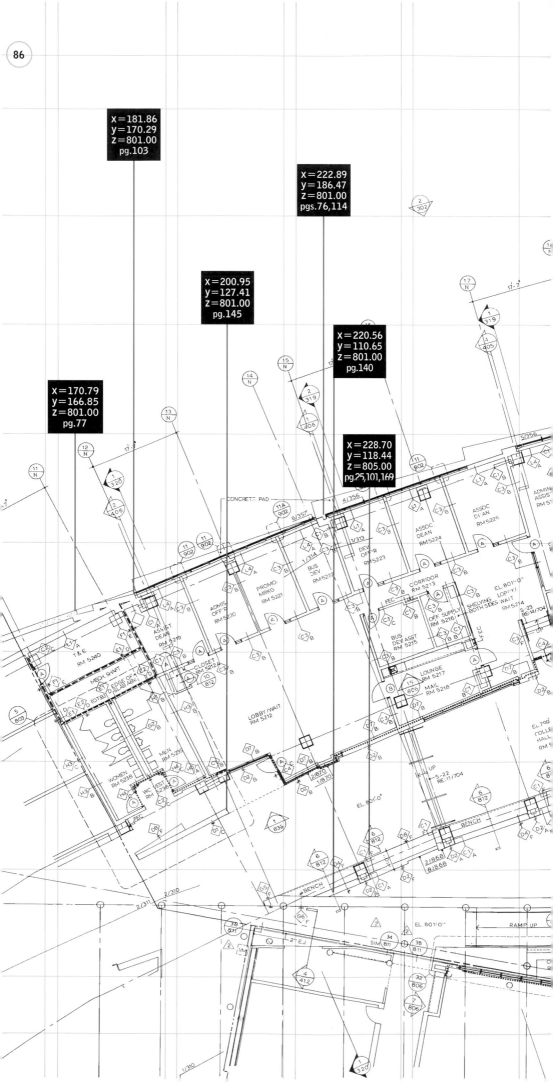

x=181.86
y=170.29
z=801.00
pg.103

x=222.89
y=186.47
z=801.00
pgs.76,114

x=200.95
y=127.41
z=801.00
pg.145

x=220.56
y=110.65
z=801.00
pg.140

x=170.79
y=166.85
z=801.00
pg.77

x=228.70
y=118.44
z=805.00
pg.25,101,169

x=310.74
y=218.66
z=801.00
pg.178

x=323.77
y=110.65
z=804.50
pg.148

x=280.05
y=113.63
z=801.00
pgs.94,181

x=323.77
y=110.65
z=801.00
pg.150

x=323.77
y=225.41
z=801.00
pg.75

x=280.77
y=100.65
z=801.00
pg.173

500 Level
NC Plan

CONCRETE PAD

FEC

VEST. C-2
RM 5207

WORKROOM
RM 5205

RM 5211
ASSIST.
DIR

ADMIN ASST
RM 5210

DIRECTOR
RM 5209

CORRIDOR
RM 5204

DEAN
OFF
RM 529

CONFERENCE RM
RM 5208

KITCH
5233

W.C.
5231

RE 13/806
FOR ELEVATION

EL. 801'-0"

UP
S-21
RE:10/704

S-1
RE: 5/704
UP

CONFERENCE RM
RM 5234

DEAN'S GAL
RM 5235

FEC

EL 796'-6"

ALIGN

UP

EL. 798'-0"
S-22
RE:11/704

S-22
RE:11/704

BENCH

RAMP

SIM

(OPEN TO
BELOW)

BENCH

LANDING
EL. 798'-0"
UP

RAMP

(OPEN TO BELOW)

2'-0"

EL. 799'-6"

CAFE
RM 5202
(OPEN TO
ABOVE)

A-111   A-110
17'-7"
17'-7"

x=263.7
y=128.7
z=811.8
pg.128

x=224.20
y=110.65
z=808.50
pg.146

OPEN TO ABOVE
RM 5201

SEE ATRIUM SKYLIGHT
DETAILS ON SHT A608

x=323.77
y=146.95
z=815.84
pg.146

x=335.87
y=159.24
z=813.49
pgs.96,144

x=304.41
y=139.59
z=818.66
pg.124

500 Level
NC Reflected
Ceiling Plan

See Barry on "laser transit method of triangulation" page 58

500 Level NC
Coordinate
Dimension Plan

x=133.18
y=153.22
z=816.50
pg.77

x=93.42
y=67.15
z=820.60
pg.165

x=112.12
y=80.30
z=820.00
pg.164

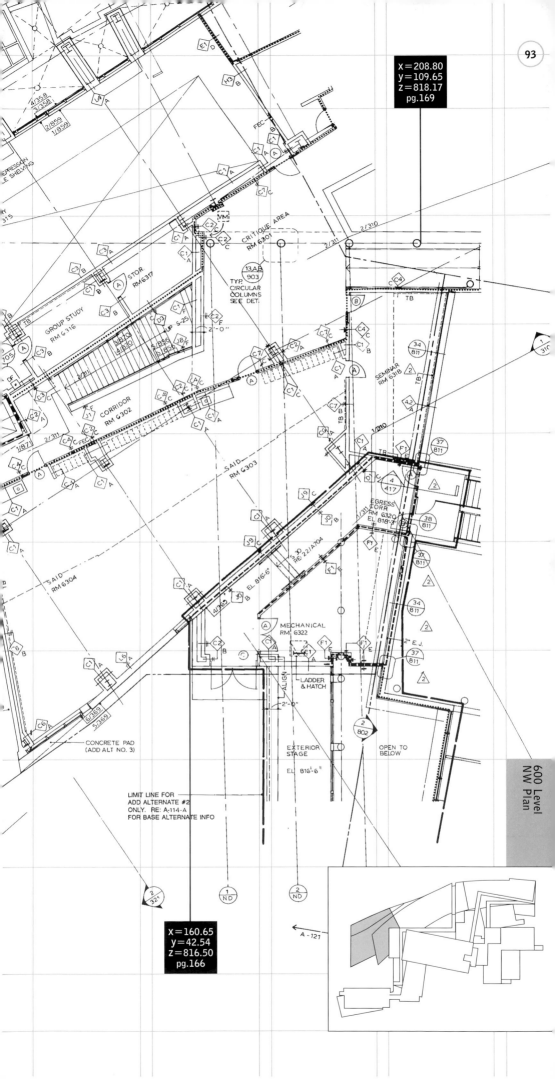

x=208.80
y=109.65
z=818.17
pg.169

x=160.65
y=42.54
z=816.50
pg.166

600 Level
NW Plan

CRITIQUE AREA
RM 6301

13.A.B
903

TYP.
CIRCULAR
COLUMNS
SEE DET.

STOR
RM 6317

GROUP STUDY
RM 6316

TB

CORRIDOR
RM 6302

FEC

SAID
RM 6303

SAID
RM 6304

SEMINAR
RM 6318

TB

EGRESS CORR
RM 6320
EL 818'-3"

MECHANICAL
RM 6322

LADDER
& HATCH

ALIGN

2'-0"

CONCRETE PAD
(ADD ALT NO. 3)

EXTERIOR
STAGE

EL 816'-6"

OPEN TO
BELOW

LIMIT LINE FOR
ADD ALTERNATE #2
ONLY. RE: A-114-A
FOR BASE ALTERNATE INFO

2" E.J.

A-121

2/310

1/310

34
811

37
811

38
811

3X
811

34
811

37
811

4
417

2
802

EL 816'-6"

2'-0"

SJO
RE 22/A704

x=280.05
y=133.63
z=801.00

Go to
500 Level NC Plan
page 87

A NOTE ON THE CRIMINOLOGY OF ORNAMENT: FROM SULLIVAN TO EISENMAN

Henry N. Cobb

A brief glimpse into a small fragment of a still incomplete and densely scaffolded interior space can scarcely be said to constitute an adequate basis for comment on a work of architecture. Nonetheless I am incautious enough to affirm that during a hurried tour in January 1996 of Peter Eisenman's Aronoff Center for Design and Art (an addition to the College of Design, Architecture, Art, and Planning at the University of Cincinnati), I discerned therein — not without some astonishment — irrefutable evidence of that rarest of inventions, a new system of architectural ornament.

My use of the words that Louis Sullivan chose as the title of his last, posthumously published monograph is no accident. For however unlikely it may seem, Eisenman's ornament, though executed entirely in gypsum wallboard, shares with Sullivan's a trait that Frank Lloyd Wright most admired in his Lieber Meister's terra cotta exfoliations: the elimination of background. Thus in the Aronoff Center, Elsenman has impenitently reintroduced a topic that has been largely neglected — one might almost say that it has been a taboo — in 20th-century architectural discourse. Setting aside Adolf Loos's polemical attack published in 1908 under the title Ornament and Crime, the most recent essay articulating a practical theory of architectural ornament seems to have been Sullivan's eloquent paean to Ornament in Architecture of 1892. In this paper Sullivan wrote that "a building which is truly a work of art (and I consider none other) is in its nature, essence and physical being an emotional expression. This being so, and I feel deeply that it is so, it must have, almost literally, a life. It follows from this living principle that an ornamented structure should be characterized by this quality, namely, that the same emotional impulse shall flow throughout harmoniously into its varied forms of expression of which, while the mass-composition is the more profound, the decorative ornamentation is the more intense. Yet both must spring from the same source of feeling."

What I saw at the Aronoff Center perfectly conforms to this prescription. Moreover, the building manifests in its ornamental system the same "figure/figure"

The elimination
of background

See Zaera-Polo on "a dialogue of figure/figure" page 31

Go to 500 Level NC Reflected Ceiling Plan page 89

principle that Eisenman has lately been exploring in his work at an urban scale — most notably his competition project for the Klingelhofer Triangle in Berlin. This "figure/figure urbanism" must surely acknowledge a debt to Sullivan's "elimination of background" (so much admired by Wright) as one of its hidden yet profoundly significant sources.

x=335.87
y=159.24
z=813.49

In his preface to <u>The Grammar of Ornament</u>, first published in 1856, Owen Jones declared that "construction should be decorated. Decoration should never be constructed." The Aronoff Center emphatically refutes this proposition, and in this respect Eisenman parts company with Sullivan, who would no doubt have concurred with Jones. But Eisenman's refutation is the inescapable consequence of his distinctive form-making strategy, wherein construction as conventionally defined plays an altogether secondary role.

Eisenman's architecture results not from an idea of construction but from the construction of an idea. In this case, the idea being constructed is by nature systemic, systematic, rhythmical, dynamic — and hence inherently decorative or ornamental. Furthermore, Eisenman has chosen to give voice to this idea through the manipulation of <u>surface</u> by means of layering, folding, and inscribing. As already noted, the surfaces so ornamented are composed entirely of gypsum wallboard — a material that is, like terra cotta, qualitatively neutral, banal, inexpressive, yet rendered eloquent by Eisenman's artifice. Hence it may not be too far-fetched to understand Wright's commentary on Sullivan's use of terra cotta as being also applicable to Eisenman's use of gypsum wallboard: "We may see, for once, how completely a negative material can be appropriately brought to life by the creative spirit. It is reassuring."

In taking note of Eisenman's superficial artifice — his system of ornament — I do not mean to dismiss or devalue the vigorous spatial dynamics, the engaging fluidity and eventfulness, that characterize the interior of the Aronoff Center. I only wish to point out that in pursuing his ambitious and avowedly antihumanist ideological program, with its reference to plate tectonics, its "rocking, drifting, pulsing movements," (to quote Sanford Kwinter), its torquing solids, its wave fronts, and its phase transitions — in pursuing this program Peter Eisenman has coincidentally reinvigorated the oldest, most primitive (criminally so, according to Loos), and most innately habitual of human arts: the art of ornament. Who can foretell what "crimes" may thereby be provoked in the future practice of design, architecture, art, and planning?

See Kipnis on "staggered and shifting streams" page 179

Henry N. Cobb, formerly chairman of the Department of Architecture at Harvard's Graduate School of Design, is a principal of Pei, Cobb, Freed & Partners in New York.

BUILDING INSIDE OUT: PERSPECTIVES ON THE CONSPICUOUSLY INCONSPICUOUS

Sarah Whiting

"Monuments are so conspicuously inconspicuous," Robert Musil mused in <u>Posthumous Papers of a Living Author</u>. "There is nothing in this world as invisible as a monument. They are no doubt erected to be seen — indeed to attract attention. But at the same time they are impregnated with something that repels attention, causing the glance to roll right off, like water droplets off an oilcloth, without even pausing for a moment." Musil's articulation of a monument's dependence on both visibility and invisibility provides insight into Eisenman Architects' Aronoff Center for Design and Art, an addition to the College of Design, Architecture, Art, and Planning (DAAP) at the University of Cincinnati. But the manner by which this building meets and then actively redirects the subject's "glance" indicates a game far more complex than the mere play of water droplets off an oilcloth.

Robert Musil, "Monuments," in <u>Posthumous Papers of a Living Author</u>, translated by Peter Wortsman (Hygiene, Colorado: Eridanos Library 1987), 61.

Peter Eisenman has played with the architectural subject throughout his career in an extended match intended to draw out the subject of architecture. His house projects of the 1970s challenged architecture's traditional anthropomorphic base of reference through such representational devices as axonometric analysis — a drawing technique that positions the viewer at arm's length, thereby objectifying the architectural project. Rather than presenting the object as one sees it, the axonometric presents it to scale, extruding sectional information up from the plan in accordance with a convention that is more informative than suggestive. As Yve-Alain Bois notes in writing about El Lissitzky's use of axonometry, the elimination of "all reference to a spectator's point of view . . . giv[es] way to an ambiguity that would force the spectator to make constant decisions about how to interpret what he or she sees: is this figure hollow or in relief?" In contrast to the axonometric technique of parallel projection, the more dominant architectural graphic tradition of central projec-

Yve-Alain Bois, "El Lissitzky: Radical Reversibility," in <u>Art in America</u> (April 1988), 172.

tion, or perspective, <u>depends</u> on the line of vision from the viewer's eye for its construction, and thereby introduces a subjective — even narrative — component into the architecture's documentation. The perspective image tells the object through the eyes of the spectator, and therefore the spectator's <u>perspective</u> necessarily reforms the object. Monuments, to return to Musil's speculations, depend on perspective; sightlines orchestrate their siting. This specular observation is neatly demonstrated in Baron Haussmann's rebuilding of Paris one hundred years ago: he placed all major public institutions at the ends of newly constructed boulevard axes. Each axis forms a perfect one-point perspective, with the major boulevards setting up the primary, frontal view of any particular monument. In short, the publicness of 19th-century Paris is entirely perspectival. Haussmann's tactics suggest that the city's urban, public, and institutional realms depend on subjective narration to measure or demonstrate their efficacy.

Expanding this urban logic, one might also say that by contributing to the creation of a narrative, perspective helps to create and support a political ideology. If ideology is, <u>grosso modo</u>, understood to be the system of signs and ideas that bind a social group together, either at the scale of a nation or a scout troop, then perspective (and other narrative forms) plays a crucial role in establishing and maintaining belief in that particular system. Again, Haussmann's Paris, which foregrounded particular national institutions, concretizing and aggrandizing the cultural milieu of Napoleon III's Second Empire, illustrates this point. In the history of aesthetics, such an understanding of perspective reveals a powerful intersection of formalism and ideology. Whereas Germanic formalist aesthetics, beginning with Immanuel Kant and threading through the aesthetic investigations of Robert Vischer, Conrad Fiedler, Heinrich Wölfflin, Adolf Göller, Adolf Hildebrand, and August Schmarsow, primarily focuses on the individual subject's empathetic response to form, this thread has an intersubjective component to it as well. Although Kant distinguished ethical from aesthetic judgments, he believed that aesthetic taste develops a frame of mind that ensures a moral good will. As such, Kant's aesthetic formalism was integrative: art leads to moral agency, which in turn underpins political agency.

See <u>Empathy, Form and Space: Problems in German Aesthetics 1873–1893</u>, edited by Harry Francis Mallgrave and Eleftherios Ikonomou (Santa Monica: Getty Center for the History of Art and the Humanities, 1994), for primary readings, as well as an extended analysis of this thread.

Go to
wire frame
page 38

Using axonometry, Eisenman's early house projects questioned the singular relationship between form and the individual subject. His more recent publicly scaled projects have provided a means for expanding this research to the level of intersubjectivity. I would argue that the Aronoff Center comments on the perspectival tradition underpinning public institutions and ideologies, and in so doing, successfully recasts Musil's conspicuously inconspicuous.

In his introduction to the exhibition catalogue Cities of Artificial Excavation, Jean-François Bédard groups phases of Eisenman's work according to the architect's drawing methods. Significantly, these different manners of representation correspond to a programmatic shift from the theorized isolated object to the realized urban project. The first phase, during which Eisenman investigated architecture through the house, is defined by axonometry; the second phase, consisting of the scaling projects (or cities of artificial excavation), appears in plan; and the most recent phase is investigated via the computer. The Aronoff Center is at the threshold of the third phase: computer-generated wire frames served as underlays for hand-drawn plans, elevations, sections, and perspectives, which, overlaid onto the "pure" geometries of the computer diagrams, provide the more "experiential" geometries of material conditions for details such as mullions. In more recent projects by Eisenman Architects, the combination of these pure and experiential geometries has been done with the computer. In these projects, the architect's previously signature axonometrics have been replaced by perspectives that take the viewer through the projects' ever more complex geometries. I would argue, however, that the critical strategy of axonometry has never been relinquished over the course of Eisenman's career. The ghost of axonometry's intention continues to infiltrate both the hand-drawn perspectives of the Aronoff Center and the computer-generated perspectives of more recent work, shifting these perspectives from the centralized instruments of authority á la Haussmann to the provocative ambiguity of El Lissitzky.

Eisenman claims in the project description that "we worked together with the students, faculty, administrators, and friends of the College so that the building was not a monument to architecture," but such efforts to avoid the form of conventional monumentality belie

Jean-François Bédard, ed., Cities of Artificial Excavation: The Work of Peter Eisenman, 1978–1988, (Canadian Centre for Architecture, Montréal/Rizzoli International), 9–18.

an altogether different monumentality inside the building. How can an addition that doubles the size of an institutional building, and that is also symbolic of the discipline of architecture, not become a monument of some sort? As with most of Eisenman's statements, the claim of nonmonumentality should be understood as a reflection on architecture itself — on the conventions and practices that are typically sustained in architecture, inconspicuous, uninterrupted, and unquestioned. At the Aronoff Center, this inconspicuous side to architecture, the invisibly monumental, is rendered conspicuous or apparent.

Eisenman critiques monumentality through form without forming the monumental. Instead of prescribing or narrating a singular "glance," the project allows for a multiplicity of "glancing" possibilities. Through form he recasts the role of perspective as a multicentering device, and in so doing places the occupant of the Aronoff Center into an oscillating relationship with an infinite number of vanishing points. Rather than create an object that can be recognized on axis and then classified typologically in the mindless mental gesture that renders the spectator blind to the monument, this building is de-objectified through a strategy of indeterminate multivalency that blurs the boundary between site and building. This blurring exploits what Musil considers to be the monument's moment of weakness: "Monuments always fall short. They repel the very thing they are supposed to attract. One cannot say we did not notice them; one would have to say they 'de-notice' us, they elude our perceptive faculties: this is a downright vandalism-inciting quality of theirs!" The design of the Aronoff Center deliberately encourages this de-noticing; as Eisenman explains, "Our idea in the design process was to have the building develop from within

This question of the monumental, or, more generally, of the dilemmas raised by trying to maintain Eisenman's theoretical intentions within his built work, has been at the heart of many recent discussions of his executed projects. For a particularly pertinent parallel to the discussion of the Aronoff Center, see Anthony Vidler's "Counter-Monuments in Practice: The Wexner Center for the Visual Arts," which engages these questions in relation to another academic institutional project [published in Wexner Center for the Visual Arts, The Ohio State University (New York: Rizzoli, 1989), 32–37].

See Kolbowski on "denial of the ceremonial" page 140

x=263.17
y=131.90
z=749.50

Go to 500 Level NC Plan page 86

Musil, op cit., 62.

the place itself — the site, the existing building, and the spirit of the college; in a sense the work was to find the building in the site. Its vocabulary came from the curves of land forms and the chevron forms of the existing building setting up a dynamic relationship to organize the space between the two."

Peter Eisenman, "College of Design, Architecture, Art, and Planning: University of Cincinnati," in Architecture + Urbanism (January 1990), 162.

Go to aerial view page 47

Top view, presentation model, 1989

The campus on which the project is sited is itself dynamic; individual buildings are scattered as independent pieces, not as interdependent parts forming a coherent whole. The campus appears to be unified only through a dense common infrastructure of parking garages, which, although stylistically different, instill on the campus an outwardly visible programmatic consistency that echoes the programmatic catacombs of the academy's inner workings. In the Aronoff Center, this campuswide atomization is converted to a series of transitions: entities give way to reverberations as if the heaviness of the innumerable, fully packed parking garages had caused the ground to shift. Indeed, this project marks a shift away from the archaeological projects (highlighted in the "Cities of Artificial Excavation" exhibition at the Canadian Centre for Architecture in 1994) and toward a more geological sensibility that relies on theories of plate tectonics in order to predict and understand the effect of deformations caused by the internal movements of geological masses — or, in this project, of the chevron found in the relationship of the original three DAAP buildings.

The architectural tectonic — a metaphor taken from geology that over time has acquired its own architectural status as the interplay of surface and structure — is here folded back into the primary meaning of tectonic, which the dictionary defines as "relating to the deformation of the crust of a moon or planet (as earth), the forces involved in or producing such deformation, and the resulting forms." Rather than blurring the boundary between site and building through extreme contextualization, the project recontextualizes the site through such tectonic means.

The landscape strategy for the Aronoff Center emanates from the original DAAP buildings: the chevrons derived from those buildings are extended over the site's contours like kudzu vines reclaiming the site's traditional status as origin. Unlike conventional institutional buildings whose sites serve as plinths to accentuate the institution's literal and metaphorical height over its surroundings, here it is difficult to discern whether the building is emerging from its landscape or whether the landscape is engulfing the building. There is no single vantage point from which to view and thereby apprehend the entire building. The whole constitutes a scaleless, directionless, ungraspable form that cannot be read from the outside in; instead, its enigmatic, particularly engaging east elevation, or entry facade, simultaneously promises the possibility and demands the necessity of multiple readings from the inside out.

x=181.86
y=170.29
z=801.00

Go to
500 Level NC Plan
page 86

See Forster on
"burrowing into the sloping contour"
page 114

If the exterior has been rendered inconspicuous by blurring the distinction between nature and building, the interior — normally a building's most inconspicuous or invisible realm — here receives a heightened significance. In short, the Aronoff Center has been turned inside out. The monumentality that has been dissolved on the outside appears instead on the inside, albeit in unconventional ways. The inside is not made monumental by aggrandizing the interior space in the form of a singular interiorized figure. Such an "atrium strategy" is employed, for example, in John Portman's Renaissance Center in Detroit,

which, like the Aronoff Center is meant to be read not as an exterior object but as an interior space. But while Renaissance Center — or any number of atrium-organized buildings — uses its interior monumentality as a singular, constant reference point for its users, the Aronoff Center manipulates this space to reference architecture's inherent multiplicity.

Go to
400 Level NE Plan
page 80

x=361.98
y=169.91
z=791.00

The Aronoff "atrium" forms, according to the project description, "a large multi-purpose College Hall . . . created as a symbolic shared space for juries and exhibitions." This shared space, which will also include a café at the 400 level, serves as a programmatic but not formal focal point for the Aronoff. The traditional strategy of a central space is formally altered here by drawing this space through the building rather than positioning it in one location. Branching away from the irregular volume of the café level is a grand stair that climbs the entire length of the addition, providing jury and exhibition spaces on its broad landings. The café space, which occupies the residual space between the original DAAP buildings and the new addition, initially appears to play the role of atrium by negotiating the zone between the old and the new, but it is the stair that allows the entire addition to be understood as a space of negotiation. Like the monumental stairs of S. Maria Maggiore in Rome, the Grand Stair of Garnier's Opéra in Paris, or even the steps of the Metropolitan Museum in New York, this grand stair creates a public space in which to see and be seen. But where these traditional public stairs allow for an expanded, omnipotent visual field — at any moment one can see the entire stair as well as the entire space in which it is placed — the Aronoff's jury/exhibition space constantly frustrates such a simultaneously controlled and open-ended viewpoint. Rather than providing a singular spatial figure or a singular stage on which to focus, the building's interior offers a series of echoing figures, a series of points that multiply the view. The sweeping perspective suggested by the grand stair is never fulfilled, but rather is constantly challenged by cross-axial views onto

College Hall. Although the stair draws the eye upward
in a seemingly direct line, it actually wraps to the left
in a slow curve that keeps the end always "around the
bend." The seemingly final bend is further obscured by
a bridge that subordinates the central axis to its cross
axis right where the central moment of culmination
should be. These overlapping and manipulated
perspectives create the a-prescriptive quality of
the space.

Several other cross axes question the primacy of the
central perspective even before this indeterminate
endpoint. The transverse connections serve as
bridges, cutting across the building's deformed linearity to join the addition to the original buildings.
Other axes are purely visual: views into the offices on
one side of the grand stair, or across the central space
to the original buildings, or down to the café. From
the building's entrance all the way to the nonexistent
culmination of the bent axis, vanishing points migrate
up and down as well as laterally. Unlike an atrium,
where the bottom level has the greatest floor plate
and all higher levels look down onto it, here there is
no level from which the entire central space can be
assessed. These vertical and horizontal cross views
consistently interrupt the "symbolic shared space,"
rendering that symbol ambiguous; they suggest other,
multiple programmatic relations among the building's varied constituencies of students, faculty, and
administration, but they also create anxieties. There
is always the promise or glimpse of something to hear
or see in an adjacent space. Similarly, there is the
omnipresent sense that others can glimpse or see you
from other spaces. The curve of the main stair and the
numerous vertical and horizontal cross axes and
planes create an infinite number of vanishing points;
there is no "correct" point from which to view. Even
in the main auditorium, the central view onto the
stage is distracted: mysterious and alluring balcony
spaces pull the eye upward and out; slits of fluorescent lighting follow the chevron in the ceiling, suggesting not only the original buildings but also the
possibility of a light space directly above; and, final-

See Kwinter on "channeling
on the way to somewhere"
page 158

Go to
central space
page 128

Go to
balcony
page 130

x=432.66
y=200.28
z=807.00

Go to
500 Level NE Reflected Ceiling Plan
page 85

ly, the angled planes — neither parallel nor converging — that form the walls of the auditorium draw the eye in innumerable directions. Surpassing the postmodern textual critiques that dismantled such central, omnipotent viewpoints, this project constructs multiple centers which, when seen from multiple vantage points, create multiple repercussions in the form of a built critique.

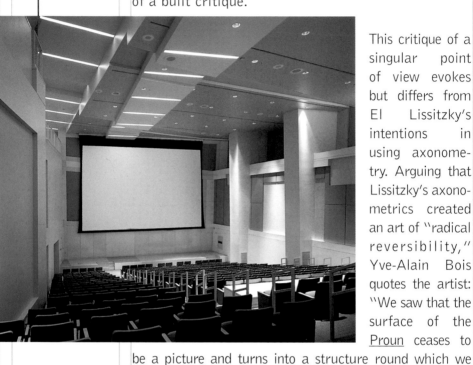

This critique of a singular point of view evokes but differs from El Lissitzky's intentions in using axonometry. Arguing that Lissitzky's axonometrics created an art of "radical reversibility," Yve-Alain Bois quotes the artist: "We saw that the surface of the Proun ceases to be a picture and turns into a structure round which we must circle, looking at it from all sides, peering down from above, investigating from below. The result is that the one axis of the picture which stood at right angles to the horizontal was destroyed. Circling round it, we screw ourselves into the space. . . . We have set the Proun in motion so we obtain a number of axes of projection." As Bois notes, the elimination of the primary visual axis pulls the viewer's own coordinates out from under him or her: "The viewer should no longer have a base of operations, but must be made continually to choose the coordinates of his or her visual field, which therefore become variable."

Bois, op cit., 174.

Ibid.

But while Lissitzky's Prouns remain objects and the desired effect of alienation remains an exterior condition, Eisenman's Aronoff Center manipulates the coordinates of the viewer while allowing him or her to enter the space itself. Rather than abandon perspective for axonometry, Eisenman here "axonometricizes" perspective itself to create a sublime, interiorized landscape entirely inconspicuous from the building's exterior. The indeterminacy and critical ambiguity of axonometry here become experiential. Seen in perspective, Eisenman's project significantly reworks the cool detachment of axonometry's "objectivity." Here, "screwing oneself into space" is a deliberate act of engagement in contrast to a disinterested glance. By constructing perspective as a critical device rather than as a device that merely endorses ideologies by prescribing specific viewpoints, Eisenman encourages the spectator to interpret for himself or herself not just the architecture but also the relationships among the users of the building.

Conspicuously inconspicuous, the impact and scale of the building occur on the inside, not the outside. The Aronoff Center does not sit as an institutional power dominating its landscape, but suggests through its form and programming many reciprocal relationships between landscape and building, institution and constituents, ideology and critique, perspective and axonometry, original and new. Meeting the monumental challenge of building a public institution, Eisenman redefines the monumental by redefining the architectural device of the perspective to engage rather than prescribe.

See Hays on "it is all interior" page 25

The extent to which that engagement can have an effect, however, runs the risk of being countered by its material permanence. As Musil notes, the paradox of monuments is that "anything that endures over time sacrifices its ability to make an impression. Anything that constitutes the walls of our life, the backdrop of our consciousness, so to speak, forfeits its capacity to play a role in that consciousness." It would be unrealistic to assume that because it elicits multiple narratives from its subjects rather than forcing a singular narrative upon them, the Aronoff Center will overcome this paradox with ease. At the same time, it is precisely such engaged intersubjectivity that sets up the possibility of some significant shifts in the way that this building might be interpreted, occupied, and worn. The ceaseless flux of students will engage this interior each year, each quarter, and the somewhat less fluid, but still mobile flow of faculty, staff, and administrators will engage it in other ways. These multiple, mutable perspectives ultimately do form the basis of a monumentality, albeit a monumentality of flux and possibility rather than one of stasis and memory.

Musil, op cit., 62.

Sarah Whiting is a Ph.D. candidate in the History, Theory, and Criticism of Art, Architecture, and Urban Form program at the Massachusetts Institute of Technology, and is review editor of Assemblage.

x=419.31
y=124.08
z=794.00

Go to
300 Level NE Plan
page 78

300 Level
Entrance

x=429.98
y=119.20
z=773.50

Connecting chevron passes
over entrance hall

x=434.61
y=137.40
z=773.50

Go to
300 Level NE Plan
page 78

View from 400 Level
chevron "bridge" down to 300 Level

x=381.42
y=111.19
z=773.50

Go to
300 Level NE Plan
page 78

300 Level

EXIT

x=382.53
y=117.54
z=795.80

Go to
400 Level NE Reflected Ceiling Plan
page 82

x=345.25
y=113.95
z=773.50

Go to
300 Level NE Plan
page 78

300 Level

300 Level looking up
at 400 Level chevron connector

RISING FROM THE LAND, SINKING INTO THE GROUND

Kurt W. Forster

Peter Eisenman's project for the new Aronoff Center for Design and Art at the University of Cincinnati has been widely known since it shared the American pavilion at the 1991 Venice Biennale with Frank Gehry's project for the Walt Disney Concert Hall. A close inspection of Eisenman's plans causes one to puzzle endlessly over the intricate mesh of lines that makes up the design. Even the experience of a visit to the construction site this year, where one could ponder the structure as it was completed, does not readily translate into words. Knowledge of Eisenman's other buildings is also of little avail in trying to grasp the lines of thought that run through this work. Its most striking features all derive from conceptions of motion and inertia: an unfamiliar delicacy of surface oddly suspending the momentous forces that are awakened within the building's lumbering frame, or, say, a grand sweep like that of a reptilian body pressing itself into the jagged contours of the neighboring structure while burrowing into the sloping contour of the site.

Go to 500 Level NC Plan page 86

x=222.89
y=186.47
z=801.00

The Greater Columbus Convention Center in Ohio was probably the first building of Eisenman's to signal an altogether new departure (although out of sequence,

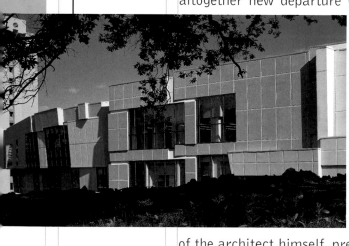

because it was built before but conceived after the Aronoff Center), raising fresh ideas about what a building might be, not just by itself but within its immediate setting as well as beyond its physical boundaries. Yet no amount of preparation, not even the prompting of the architect himself, prepared me for the reality of the Aronoff Center in Cincinnati. Nearly a decade after it was first developed, the actual encounter with its built reality displaces the project from its chronological station in the architect's oeuvre. A visit to the site is a bit like opening a long-lost letter which discloses events that have not yet occurred.

Rising from the Land,
Sinking into the Ground
Kurt W. Forster

The delay in construction is not the only explanation for the chronological conundrum one faces in Cincinnati: Eisenman has always pursued the potential of his ideas as far as their legs would take them. For this reason, a building emerging out of sequence in relation to his current work requires an act of reorientation. I do not imply that we are looking at an outdated building, but its date within the trajectory of Eisenman's thinking is now "out of place" with regard to its chronology. Far from being a handicap, this circumstance adds yet another dimension to our experience, insofar as an odd familiarity resonates within the building's striking newness. Moreover, because the Aronoff Center is nearly the only project to have actually been built out of a clutch of comparable projects dating from the 1980s, its construction now establishes a single, if disjointed, point of reference for Eisenman's other campus projects. Its belated appearance "in the flesh" therefore provokes reactions quite different from those it would have prompted years ago, and, conversely, by virtue of its appearance after the architect's most recent projects, the Center opens up a startlingly different vantage point on his ideas.

The tightrope tension holding idea and building together has always endowed Eisenman's architecture with a conjectural ambition that few architects dare entertain today. This conjectural dimension has kept his work from congealing within its own logic and has instead opened it up for a future, a future whose aspiration one senses almost as forcefully as the draft in an unoccupied edifice. Such conjectures — Le Corbusier stashed them in his familiar formulation about architecture as "speculation" on itself — have a life of their own. To explore their ramifications is like climbing a tree to test its resilience, or, as I have put it elsewhere, Eisenman's architectural conjectures work like hypothesis. The difference between a scientific hypothesis and an architectural conjecture lies perhaps in the peculiar nature of architecture itself. In a building, ideas need to locate themselves in, as well as stand against, the physical structure. For this reason, projects are not so much tested against their representation on paper as against themselves in built form. Studying their plans is an act akin to silently reading a musical score rather than playing it, but once a building has been constructed, the architect's "score" takes shape in all aspects and modalities of its execution.

Cf. my "Eisenman Unfolding" in AV Monografías 53 (1995), 10–19.

Among Eisenman's works of the 1980s, the most complex in concept, and the most intriguing in their exfoliation, were the campus projects. From the Wexner Center at The Ohio State University, and the Art Museum at California State University, Long Beach, to the Biocentrum at Frankfurt, the Carnegie-Mellon Research Institute, and the Emory Center for the Arts, these projects became the testing ground of Eisenman's maturity. If private houses had been the ostensible subject of his first decade of work, campus buildings succeeded them as the sites of his invention during the 1980s. The true measure of their rupture with the ideas he established for the houses emerges in the categorical change from location to site: Eisenman's houses clove to the concept of the modernist dwelling as a deracinated object; the campus projects, on the other hand, began to dig into their sites, to extend themselves beyond their physical limits, and extend their presence to a wide web of ideas.

Eisenman pushed the process by which he generated his early houses to its internal completion, virtually driving his initial idea to the point of self-closure.

See Barry on "the illusion of movement" page 56

These houses had little specific connection to their location, but their conceptual facades remained intact as he continued the modernist search for an inner process of design that reveals itself in external manifestations. The campus projects, by contrast, were conceived largely for sites among existing buildings — like the Wexner Center. They also opened up cavities within themselves — like the Biocentrum in Frankfurt and the Carnegie-Mellon Research Institute.

After the Wexner Center, Eisenman took his work in a new direction. At the Aronoff Center he not only transposed the footprint of the adjacent building and multiplied its stepped contour, while avoiding any figurative manifestations, but he also set a curvilinear body in motion against its preexistent rectilinear neighbor. The decisive difference between this and the gridded spaces of the Wexner Center lies in the allusion to a moving body, or to a creeping flow inside the building. I recall Eisenman's off-hand remark at the time of its genesis, suggesting a similarity between airport baggage conveyors and the reptilian motion which characterizes the main building in Cincinnati. Such shorthand has its limits, but it also points up the intuitive desire — across all differences of generation and culture — for an architecture harkening to life forms (although not in

Rising from the Land,
Sinking into the Ground
Kurt W. Forster

the D'Arcy Thompson sense) rather than crystalline
geometry as its formal premise, or, to cite Le Corbusier's
note of 1952, to develop "figures toward animal
shapes which are carriers of character" and of "an
algebraic ability to enter into connection with each
other and thus release a poetic phenomenon."

On these grounds, the juxtaposition of projects by
Peter Eisenman and Frank Gehry at the Venice
Biennale revealed profound affinities in the two architects' search for buildings of such "algebraic ability."
Similarity of appearance does not always follow from
a congruence of method, even of approach. The affinity between these two buildings by Gehry and
Eisenman establishes itself on a level below the visible. They resemble less two rivers cutting their mean-
dering beds across the same valley than they correspond to each other like the surface stream to its
underground aquifer; that is to say, the visible similarities at times obscure, and at other times expose,
the nature of their connection. This connection finds
its origin in the desire of both architects to allow ideas
and intuitions to take physical shape in ways that have
not been accepted in architecture, or tolerated as
building forms, for a very long time. The Disney
Concert Hall and the Aronoff Center startle in their
wholly unexpected similarities of intent, despite the
fact that each architect arrived at his result by utter-
ly divergent processes. For both architects the instrumental, if indispensable, employment of computation-
al programs remains just that, an indispensable
means; but it holds no explanatory power over the
results. I can think of only one image for something so
defiantly set against conventional images as this
architecture, and for its inexplicably fluid emergence
from telluric slumber. It is the image Osip
Mandel'shtam drew from his memories of the French
cathedrals at Reims and Laon during his banishment
to Voronezh: "I saw the lake standing. Here before my
eyes, /A house built of its sweet water . . ."

All along, modern architecture has sought to capture a
sense of motion rather than merely suggest animation.
The sacrifice of ornament attested to a commitment to
rigor, and rendered the desire to evoke the qualities of
mobility only more intense. The articulations of this
desire, from Antonio Gaudi to Louis Sullivan and
Claude Perret, haunt modernism's strictures against
ornament like shadows: Look at the graphics of the

Le Corbusier Sketchbooks, ed. Francois de Franclieu
(New York and Cambridge, MA: The Architectural
History Foundation / MIT Press II, 1950–1954), 700.

See Kolbowski on
"legitimacy of . . . design methods"
page 137

As reported by Viveca Bosson, "Le Corbusier — the architect who became a painter and sculptor," in Le Corbusier — Painter and Architect, catalogue of the exhibition in Aalborg, Denmark, 1995, 33.

waves, the whirls of the clouds and the winds, the waterfall's paraboloid, Ozenfant reminded his friends. The classicizing stability lurking in the matrix of modern architecture would yield to an altogether different dynamic of form. Only when these flowing shapes cease to be encrustations of congealed motion do they begin to exercise a formative power on buildings themselves. In the language of ornament, these shapes merely imply a force long drained from them, but defined as force instead of form, they generate architecture from an unprecedented basis. The new fluid shapes can no longer be derived from the intricacies and geometric eccentricities of baroque symbols, nor from the expressionist will-to-form and its subjective hubris. The only

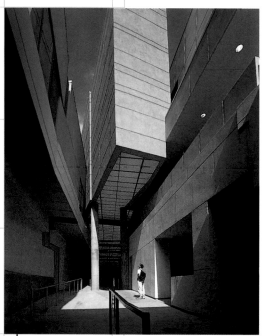

basis for these new forms of architecture — which arise from complex interdependent manifestations of motion — lies in the mental pictures of modern science.

In this respect, too, the Aronoff Center goes beyond the largely symbolic association of architectural shapes with hypothetical scientific modeling in the Biocentrum at Frankfurt. In Cincinnati, the building does not assume the appearance of a full scale kit of ready-made parts; rather it creates the impression of perpetual motion (and of parts coincident with, rather than incidental to it). Correspondingly, the impression of motion arises from the internal state of the building rather than the transitory evocation of an illusion. It is difficult to imagine anything more unavoidable in its mechanics than the collision of the old and the new wings (for lack of a better term) over the principal entrance. And the single most astonishing space ever built by Eisenman, the atrium ascending between canting walls along the central cavity of the building, exhibits such interpenetrations in its own exceptional properties. These properties derive from the fact that the atrium blends the subterranean aspect of a cryptoporticus with the ceremonial ascent of a public stairway. The skylight creates the impression of a clearing within the building; the hallway, of conduits leading through it.

Go to 300 Level NE Plan page 79

x=429.29
y=119.64
z=785.50

Along a curving pathway that begins at a parking area below and rises toward the entrance above, every volume, be it a planter or the balustrade or a

119

Rising from the Land,
Sinking into the Ground
Kurt W. Forster

classroom high above eye level, submits to otherwise invisible forces, shifting, twisting, and sliding out of level and plumb. To enter the building is to slip under it, through the door beneath a brightly lit wedge of an overhang, only to begin rising, again, seemingly from a level even farther below than where one began. The core of the building stands one's spatial expectation on its head: at the end of a long, halting, and curving climb through the core of the building, one finds one-self no higher than the street level of the campus avenue on the other side of the building. The pro-longed ascent through a cavernous atrium, beginning well below grade and ending just at ground level, has a curious effect. Our conventional notion of ascent and descent yields to the powerful kinetic experience of the continuous climb as a descent into the depth of the building.

This parcours throughout the building amounts to a virtually Piranesian feat, pulled off with appropriate-ly baroque daring. The curious alloy of spatial proper-ties and sequential reversals bring to mind a peculiar form of tribute that architects of the 17th century were paid for such inventive transpositions: "As you enter the structure, you behold an immense colonnade, and with a few steps put it behind you; what is distant appears the larger for it, but once newer, turns small . . . A stupendous artifice, and an image of fallacious reality . . . in which small things are made to reveal big ones. On earth, bigness remains a treacherous phantom."

See Kwinter on
"the highly sought Piranesi effect"
page 161

The passage through the Aronoff Center leads to a sudden encounter with the inside of the beast. Here it is not the building's expansive vol-umetric presence, its "bigness," but its "treacherous" and hidden nature that descends upon visitors and engulfs them in a cavernous space. The delicate hues, inside and out, quite innocently resemble the tonalities of the rococo, but they did not fail then, and will not today, to adumbrate — as they dissimulate — darker regions of the imagination. After all, elegance and refinement did not prevent Mozart from breaking the crust of the earth with the sound of trombones announcing the commendatore's return.

Epigram by Cardinal Bernardino Spada in praise of the architect's con-ceit for the perspectival colonnade in the garden of the Roman Palazzo Spada, attributed to Borromini, cited after Biblioteca Apostolica Vaticana, Barb. cat. 1005, c.102, in: Lionello Neppi, Palazzo Spada (Rome, 1972), Doc. 7. The relevant passages in the original Latin read: "Mole sub exigua spectatur porticus ingens;/ Cernitur in spatio semita lunga brevi:/ Quoque magis distant tanto maiora videntur/Quae sunt in proprio corpora parva loco. / Artis opus mirae; mundis fallenti imago; . . . Grandia sub coelo non nisi spectra marent."

Kurt W. Forster,
founding director of the
Getty Research Center
for the History of Art
and the Humanities
(1984-1992), is
professor of the History
and Theory of
Architecture at the
Federal Institute of
Technology in Zurich,
Switzerland.

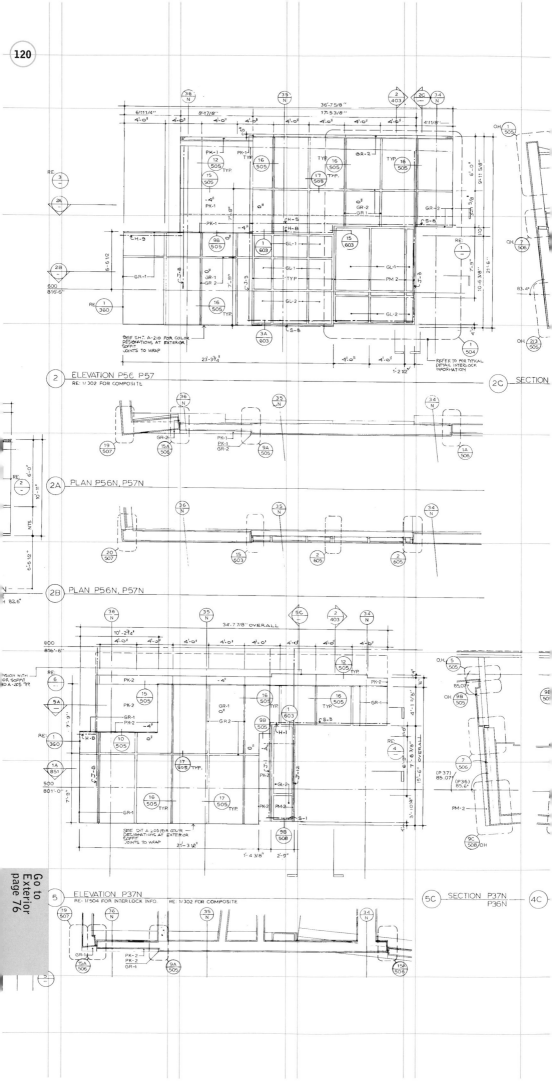

Go to
Exterior
page 76

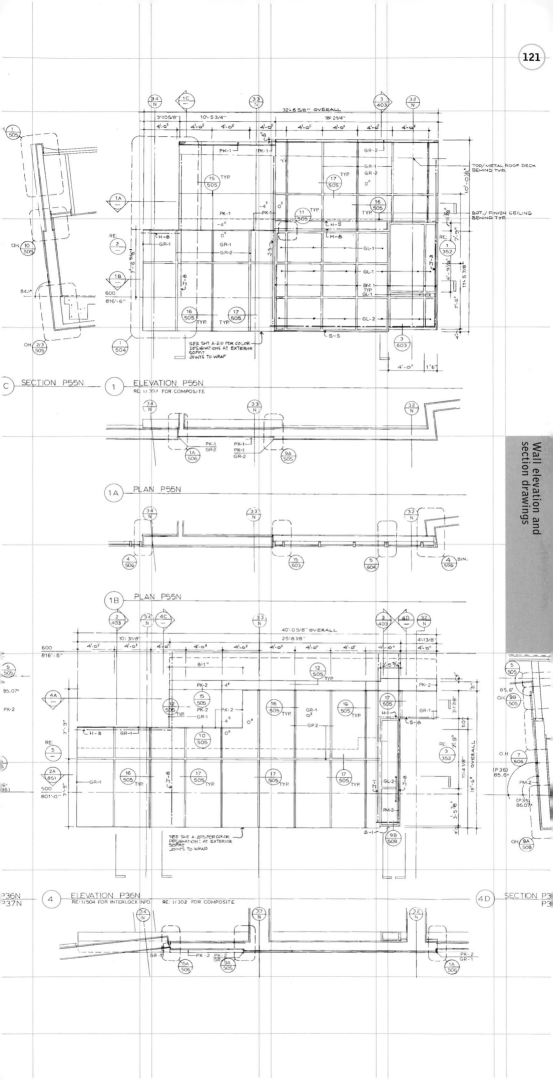

Wall elevation and section drawings

SECTION P55N

1 ELEVATION P55N
RE: 1/302 FOR COMPOSITE

1A PLAN P55N

1B PLAN P55N

4 ELEVATION P36N
P36N
P37N
RE: 1/504 FOR INTERLOCK INFO   RE: 1/302 FOR COMPOSITE

4D SECTION P3
P3

SEE SHT A-210 FOR COLOR
DESIGNATIONS AT EXTERIOR
SOFFIT
JOINTS TO WRAP

SEE SHT A-205 FOR COLOR
DESIGNATIONS AT EXTERIOR
SOFFIT
JOINTS TO WRAP

TOP/METAL ROOF DECK
BEHIND TYP.

BOT./FINISH CEILING
BEHIND TYP.

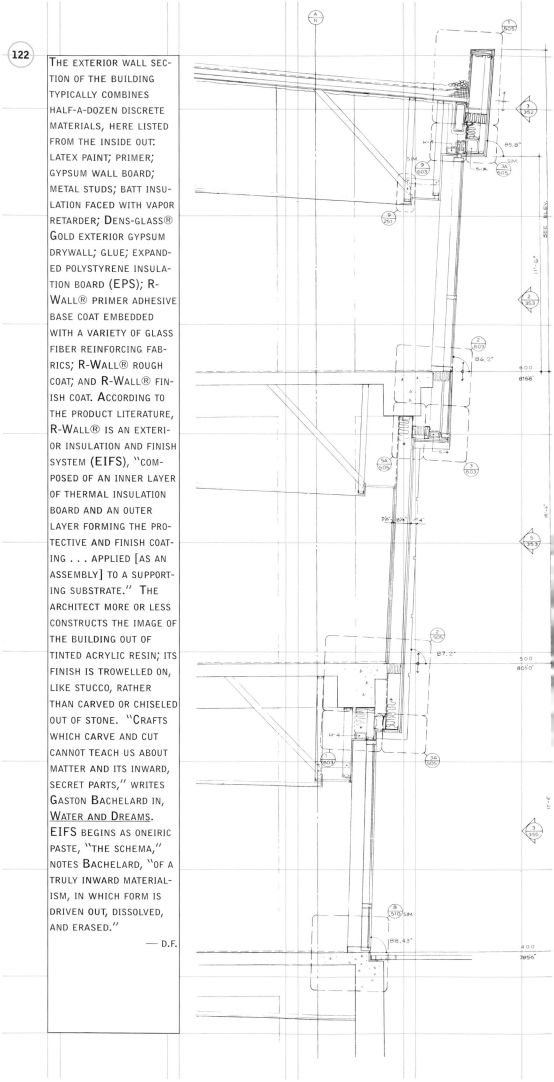

THE EXTERIOR WALL SEC-
TION OF THE BUILDING
TYPICALLY COMBINES
HALF-A-DOZEN DISCRETE
MATERIALS, HERE LISTED
FROM THE INSIDE OUT:
LATEX PAINT; PRIMER;
GYPSUM WALL BOARD;
METAL STUDS; BATT INSU-
LATION FACED WITH VAPOR
RETARDER; DENS-GLASS®
GOLD EXTERIOR GYPSUM
DRYWALL; GLUE; EXPAND-
ED POLYSTYRENE INSULA-
TION BOARD (EPS); R-
WALL® PRIMER ADHESIVE
BASE COAT EMBEDDED
WITH A VARIETY OF GLASS
FIBER REINFORCING FAB-
RICS; R-WALL® ROUGH
COAT; AND R-WALL® FIN-
ISH COAT. ACCORDING TO
THE PRODUCT LITERATURE,
R-WALL® IS AN EXTERI-
OR INSULATION AND FINISH
SYSTEM (EIFS), "COM-
POSED OF AN INNER LAYER
OF THERMAL INSULATION
BOARD AND AN OUTER
LAYER FORMING THE PRO-
TECTIVE AND FINISH COAT-
ING . . . APPLIED [AS AN
ASSEMBLY] TO A SUPPORT-
ING SUBSTRATE." THE
ARCHITECT MORE OR LESS
CONSTRUCTS THE IMAGE OF
THE BUILDING OUT OF
TINTED ACRYLIC RESIN; ITS
FINISH IS TROWELLED ON,
LIKE STUCCO, RATHER
THAN CARVED OR CHISELED
OUT OF STONE. "CRAFTS
WHICH CARVE AND CUT
CANNOT TEACH US ABOUT
MATTER AND ITS INWARD,
SECRET PARTS," WRITES
GASTON BACHELARD IN,
WATER AND DREAMS.
EIFS BEGINS AS ONEIRIC
PASTE, "THE SCHEMA,"
NOTES BACHELARD, "OF A
TRULY INWARD MATERIAL-
ISM, IN WHICH FORM IS
DRIVEN OUT, DISSOLVED,
AND ERASED."

— D.F.

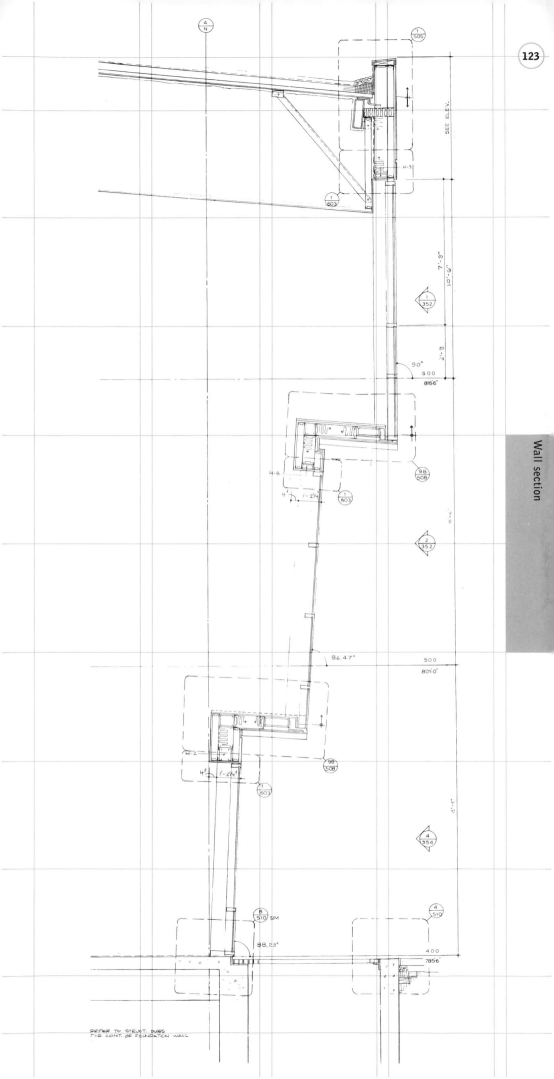

REFER TO STRUCT. DWGS
FOR CONT. OF FOUNDATION WALL

Observers on 500 Level chevron bridge look down on 400 Level central space

x=304.41
y=139.59
z=818.66

Go to
500 Level NC Reflected Ceiling Plan
page 89

400 Level

View from 400 Level
chevron bridge to
central space

Go to
opposite view
page 110

x=383.93
y=117.30
z=785.50

Go to
400 Level NE Plan
page 80

Go to
broader view
page 158

x=358.85
y=128.05
z=785.60

Go to
400 Level NE Plan
page 80

400 Level

400 Level chevron
bridge at far left,
College Hall at right

x=263.74
y=128.79
z=811.80

Go to
500 Level NC Reflected Ceiling Plan
page 88

x=334.01
y=127.70
z=785.50

Go to
400 Level NE Plan
page 80

400 Level

Skylight and light grid over
400 Level central space as seen
from 600 Level classroom

x=514.02
y=218.28
z=785.50

Go to
400 Level NE Plan
page 81

x=420.18
y=152.70
z=813.02

Go to
500 Level NE Reflected Ceiling Plan
page 85

400/500 Level

Standing room on auditorium balcony

5,100-square-foot
auditorium
seats 350

x=435.46
y=224.68
z=775.00

Go to
400 Level NE Plan
page 80

400 Level

FRINGE BENEFITS

Silvia Kolbowski

ANACLITIC TYPE
Literally, leaning-up-against type; from the Greek... I lean up against. In the first phase of their development the sexual instincts have no independent means of finding satisfaction; they do so by propping themselves upon or "leaning up against" the self-preservative instincts.

Index and Glossary, A General Selection From the Works of Sigmund Freud, edited by John Rickman, M.D., (New York: Doubleday Anchor Books, 1957), 254. This quotation is attributed to James Starchey [sic], 1921, and refers the reader to the following texts by Freud: The Origin and Development of Psychoanalysis (1909), On Narcissism: An Introduction (1914), Instincts and Their Vicissitudes (1915), and The Ego and The Id (1923).

OTHER LEANINGS

It could be said, literally, that Eisenman Architects' Aronoff Center addition to the College of Design, Architecture, Art, and Planning is a leaning-up-against type of architecture. From the approach to the entry, the addition looks as though it is actually leaning on one of the preexisting buildings. For an addition, it gets too close to the other building, hugs one of its corners with what appears to be a veneer of the material of the addition, and veneer must always lean. . . . But the addition could be said to have other leanings as well. Its design leans heavily upon the conceptual models used to generate the parti — the overlapping, torquing, shifting, and stepping of a series of forms and motifs, some of which are modified by open-ended logarithmic functions: a series of boxes forming a curve, a series of traces of the exterior outline of the three existing buildings, a series of chevrons derived from the dimensions of the major corridors in one of the preexisting buildings. In borrowing from and repeating motifs from the earlier buildings — elevation, section, and plan elements, as well as columnar structure — the

x=521.17
y=171.09
z=785.50

Go to
400 Level NE Plan
page 81

new building leans on the old. This is not the only type of architectural methodology that leans on the old. A more conventional contextualist approach to the architecture of the addition would retain and update existing proportions, or repeat and update materials and motifs. In fact, such leanings are the heart of the conventional approaches. Another type of contextualist approach would acknowledge or echo the siting or massing of preexisting architecture. In such work, these strategies would always be visually evident in the addition. The visual legibility of the more conventional methodology is crucial, because it is meant to function as a kind of reinforcement of an anterior condition, a reinforcement of that for which the condition stands. But in the Aronoff Center, the visual relation to the referent is always confounded, intentionally confounded. The resulting forms, spaces, sections, and plans — the altered traces of the older buildings — do not resemble the preexisting buildings because the generating process is propped on the pre-determined distortions of relatively simple geometric conditions. While the addition itself follows the bends and turns of the existing buildings and the contours of the site in a spectacularly parasitic manner, a gap exists for the spectator — at an experiential level — as to precisely how this was accomplished. Repeated use of the building may yield a clearer image of the relationship between old and new, but while my two walks through it allowed for a reading of processes left to their own devices and for the perception of relationships to the preexisting building, this could not be called visual legibility. This lack of legibility, the gap between process and result, is significant in that it redefines "contextualism" or site specifically in a manner that is neither historicist nor typically modernist. By integrating the different motifs of the Aronoff Center, through interweavings and overlaps which the process then mingles even further, the iconography of derivation is rendered somewhat obscure to the visitor or user, but the faithfulness is nevertheless traceable. For the visitor inclined toward architecture, the Aronoff Center builds a desire to read its generation from the drawn format. For the layperson, the inclination may be to read into what appear to be motivated permutations, but such efforts will hit a brick wall, because the building itself does not specifically yield the process of its generation. However, it is the even minimal readability of design permutations that are motivated by more than purely functional or expressive concerns

The architecture of the addition

Go to overlaps page 50

that prevents the experiental quality of the building from being reduced to that of the perception of aesthetic or formal permutations. This condition sets apart this and, for example, Eisenman Architects' Greater Columbus Convention Center and Wexner Center for the Visual Arts from those architectures which are also visually or spatially complex, but of pragmatic or formal derivation.

Paradoxically, in its rigorous adherence to the preexisting buildings and landscape, an adherence that is then radically modified, the Aronoff Center is newer than, for example, a modernist work that reinterprets and reconfigures earlier paradigms, erasing the iconographic traces of the precedent but establishing an abstract continuum for a tradition. And yet it is "older," in its perversely faithful attachment to the preexisting, than a historicist work which attempts to express its attachment to the preexisting through the use of a kind of modernized pastiche.

The Aronoff Center addition relies on the <u>over</u>determination of its design by the concepts and processes

Go to 400 Level NE Plan page 80

x=362.46
y=190.50
z=791.00

chosen to generate it. In fact, the design evolution rarely deviates from the effects of these concepts and processes, even as it manages to negotiate the complex relationships between the predetermined but unprojected evolution of spaces and the institutionally dictated program. Seen through the lens of this process, there is no hierarchy of good, better, and best spaces in the building — and no primary or secondary spaces. The spaces of circulation are no less compelling than the auditorium or display spaces; the most privileged office in the building may end up without the most picturesque view of the landscape (which may be accorded to a much smaller office down the hall). The interrelated interior forms — effects of the methodology — produce complexly overflowing spaces which spill through various floor levels. The eye can discern these spaces from many surprisingly distant vantage points, but because these spaces are sometimes eccentrically compressed —

sectionally — the sensation is not necessarily one of visual domination by the subject. The eye is free to travel through these spaces while the body is stationary, and this may be what we have come to regard as pleasurable in architecture. But the intellectual or somatic projection of the body, so common to the viewing of interconnected spaces, is not without its discomforts in looking into these often horizontally compressed and hyper-articulated spatial vignettes. Projection into and through these spaces inclines and torques the viewing body, so that traveling through this space visually is disorienting, even though the physical traversal of these spaces — less compressed in reality — is a pleasurable and fascinating experience.

The significance of a methodological reliance on overdetermination is that it can serve to point to the social determination of all architectural methodologies, however repressed they may be. The methodologies of, for example, more typical contextualist approaches are themselves socially determined, conventionalized as they are by an era's adherence to particular compositional values, definitions of beauty, creativity, ornamentation, etc. And although some design approaches are referred to as instinctual, all such processes are naturalized by conventions which privilege either the legitimacy of familiar design methods or the architect's pragmatic hand (or eye) — a little more here, a little less there. Note this description of Frank Gehry's design process for the Walt Disney Concert Hall: "As Gehry pushed, pulled, added, subtracted, changed, and relocated elements of his building, he recorded his thoughts in quick ink sketches, but, as his chief conceptual tool, he relied even more on the chunky abstract wooden blocks and cardboard slabs of tabletop model building. Combining the intuitive artist's instincts with

x=384.71
y=113.00
z=788.93

Go to
400 Level NE Plan
page 80

See Hays on
"spatial tears"
page 25

a matter-of-fact pragmatism, he eschewed a self-conscious reliance on 'theory.'" Unlike the self-preservation instincts, which can be said to be biological, the "intuitive artist's instincts" are learned at the father's knee, in that they are social rather than natural gestures.

Thomas S. Hines, "Rite of Spring: Frank Gehry and the Walt Disney Concert Hall of the Los Angeles Philharmonic," in Peter Eisenman & Frank Gehry (New York, Rizzoli International Publications, 1991). (Catalogue for the Fifth International Exhibition of Architecture of the Biennale, Giardini de Castello, Pavilion of the United States, Venice Italy.)

The instincts of self-preservation have their whole functioning preconditioned by their somatic apparatus, and their object is fixed from the start, whereas the sexual instincts are defined in the first place by a certain mode of satisfaction that to begin with is nothing but a kind of fringe benefit (<u>Lustnebengewinn</u>) derived from the operation of the instincts of self-preservation.

J. Laplanche and J.-B. Pontalis, The Language of PsychoAnalysis, translated by Donald Nicholson-Smith (New York and London: W.W. Norton & Company, 1973), 31.

FUNCTION'S FRINGES

In architectural design, the methodological approach that generates a particular form or parti can be seen as a fringe benefit of the programmatic requirements projected for the building, in the sense that nonfunctional aspects of architecture will always lean on fundamental requirements. Programs may vary from culture to culture, from use to use, but the physical housing of the body and its movements preexists as a demand. In the case of the Aronoff Center, as distinct from that of some types of design approaches, the design of the building does not develop from the functional requirements. Rather, beyond the question of determining necessary square footage, the relationship between function and its fringes is given an atypical character in that the two are intentionally <u>polarized</u> from the start. The methodology used by Eisenman Architects broadly acknowledges its debt to an <u>over</u>determination of design methodology; it even goes so far as to celebrate the coincidental forms and spaces that result from a reliance on this overdetermination. But the appearance of a will — although not necessarily a free one — is readable in terms of the inscription of intention, and of programmatic accommodation and development through, among other things, the carving out of spaces by eliminating components of an a priori system after the fact. Rather than fault this methodological approach's demand that the program be fitted into the resulting plan and sections, it is possible to regard the myriad of negotiations and decisions made as to where program will be located in the intractable effects, or how the design will prod the program into atypical locations, as indications of the social potential of such a method. This is so in the sense that these negotiations regard function in architecture as an at least partially conventionalized condition, rather than an essentialist and unalterable one. For example, the question of comfort in relation to function is often taken for granted, but its cultural aspects should be analyzed. Certainly what feels comfortable to the body in one culture feels uncomfortable in another. Eisenman Architects' method of responding to functional constraints, a method through which the making of space is always also the inscription of the compromise of an omnipresent pure method, foregrounds the cultural contingencies of function, as well as the functional demands that shape the social. In both cases, in architecture and in life, the organism has to survive adversity, but how it does so should not be taken for granted. One way in which the Aronoff Center does this is through the programming of inadvertently produced, often interstitial spaces. In Freudian theory the sexual instincts are propped on the self-preservation instincts in the sense of culture leaning on biology, of the conventionalized activity deriving its form and meaning and motivation, at least in part, from what the human organism requires for its survival. The methodology of the Aronoff Center sets up what might appear to be a new type of representation that leans on function, but, in fact, the leaning is always reciprocal in that the status of the functional in the Aronoff Center is dependent on coming into contact with the representational effects produced by the exigent design process.

The negotiations between design methodology and required program sometimes take serendipitous advantage of resulting deformations in the Aronoff

EVERYWHERE I TURN IN THIS CONSTRUCTION, THE BUILDING EXCEEDS ME. ONE NEEDN'T KNOW ITS CODES TO KNOW ITS EXCESSES. I WALK AGAINST ITS IMAGE THE WAY I WALK AGAINST CURRENTS OF AIR OR UNEVEN PLANES. "HUMAN GAIT IS, IN FACT, A CONTINUALLY ARRESTED FALLING," WRITES ERWIN W. STRAUSS IN PHENOMENOLOGICAL PSYCHOLOGY, "THEREFORE, AN UNFORESEEN OBSTACLE OR A LITTLE UNEVENNESS IN THE GROUND MAY PRECIPITATE A FALL." THIS BUILDING WANTS TO DIVIDE MY EYE FROM ITS MOORINGS AND MULTIPLY EACH ARRESTED FALL BY LAUNCHING THE EYE INTO INDETERMINATE SPACE. IT'S NO PLACE FOR AN AVERAGE ORIENTEER.
— D.F.

Fringe Benefits
Silvia Kolbowski

See Zaera-Polo on "the architecture of architecture" page 30

Center. For example, the otherwise impressive main entry stair is positioned in such a way that intervening, nonfunctional elements of some of the modified motifs block an immediate view of the stair upon entry, a view which is only revealed upon walking further through what appears to be an inexpressive foyer. From certain vantage points on the stair itself, looking back toward the entry, there is no sweeping view of the stair because that too is blocked by unavoidable sectional components. This purposeful denial of the ceremonial use of perspective can be considered unavoidable, given the

x=220.56
y=110.65
z=801.00

Go to
500 Level NC Plan
page 86

See Whiting on
"glancing possibilities"
page 101

conditions of the methodology that predetermine certain spatial divisions, or it might only masquerade as unavailability, since pragmatic accommodation does in fact take place. But this accommodation is always developed within the context of heightened resistance posed by the design method.

Would you say the fringe was made of silk? Wouldn't have no other kind but silk.

"Surrey with the Fringe on Top," music and lyrics by Rodgers & Hammerstein, from the film Oklahoma!, Magna/Rodgers & Hammerstein, directed by Fred Zimmermann, 1955.

Fringe's Functions

The propping of need on its excesses — its fringes — and vice versa, is always at play in this building, a play which is experienced in spirit if not read in letter. It could be said that the sexual instincts are to the self-preservation instincts as the fringe-on-top is to the surrey. The surrey will get you to the dance even without the addition of a fringe, but it is the fringe that makes the ride more than purely utilitarian. The fringe attracts the rider to the surrey, and gives social meaning to transportation. This is why the surrey needs the fringe, even as the fringe would not exist without the surrey. Additionally, the fringe is associated with silk, and not, for example, cotton, because while cotton and silk can both provide protection, silk <u>displays</u> that which exceeds utility and, in so doing, acknowledges a spectator. By exceeding function in particular ways, silk points to the social dimension of material, to its associative roles which may register sexuality or hierarchy.

The involuted excesses of the Aronoff Center lean on function and necessity, but they do not just frame them passively in the form of decor or in the innovative use of materials or detailing. Such uses of materials and motifs, common to much architecture today, also act to exceed functional requirements, but they still bolster the conventional relations to such requirements at an ontological level. They are the icing-on-the-cake or fringe-on-the-surrey types of architecture. The Aronoff Center is a fringe-on-the-surrey-on-the-fringe building. It can be seen as an attempt to mix things up, so that what exceeds or leans on function is never simply an appliqué or decoration that leaves the social dimension of need unquestioned. The extreme systemization of the design approach invades and agitates the program by establishing resistances to the housing of programmatic needs that are even greater than those which the needs themselves establish. This is one way to understand Eisenman Architects' apparent fickleness in moving from one methodological device or referent to another, from one project to the next. The focus is on setting up discord and resistance, rather than reforming or correcting what is deemed to fall short. This aim is more in need of an overwrought logic of any kind, than of one which proposes a particular semantic reading. I might wish for more specificity in some of the office's choices of referents — logarithmic function, DNA structure, plate formation theory, etc. — that is, for more precisely motivated <u>over</u>determinations, in that such choices might refine the critical aspects of the work. But that would add a narrative dimension which the work of the office eschews in favor of a focus on stripping bare the mechanics of design — of any program and any site — in a way that denaturalizes both the process and the results. The benefit of this is that it produces an architecture that is not only as spectacular as is much contemporary architecture, it is also an architecture that reflects on its own status.

An Eisenman Architects surrey would certainly arrive at the dance, but its fringe would not only provide protection from the sun, it would also challenge our definition of glare.

Silvia Kolbowski is an artist and writer in New York.

x=362.46
y=190.50
z=791.00

Go to
400 Level NE Plan
page 80

500 Level

See Whiting on
"multi-purpose College Hall"
page 104

x=335.87
y=159.24
z=813.49

Go to
500 Level NC Reflected Ceiling Plan
page 89

See Whiting on
"a space of negotiation"
page 104

x=200.95
y=127.41
z=801.00

Go to
500 Level NC Plan
page 86

500 Level

Library entrance to right of wall,
stair to 600 Level, beyond

Office windows, far right,
look onto College Hall

x=224.20
y=110.65
z=808.50

Go to
500 Level NC Reflected Ceiling Plan
page 88

x=323.77
y=146.95
z=815.84

Go to
500 Level NC Reflected Ceiling Plan
page 89

500 Level

See Barry on
"the 'round columns''
page 57

EXIT

x=323.77
y=110.65
z=804.50

Go to
500 Level NC Plan
page 87

500 Level

View from inside 5,100-square-foot gallery; former DAAP facade at left

x=323.77
y=110.65
z=801.00

Go to
500 Level NC Plan
page 87

500 Level

CAN ONE GO BEYOND PIRANESI? (LINER NOTES FOR A BUILDING REVISITED)

Sanford Kwinter

What can a building do? Architect and layman alike are accustomed to think in terms of shelter, artful deployments of shape, mass, and form, or symbolic statement. But the building, like the word, goes much further. A building, like a word, is a vibratory phenomenon, a resonance; it disturbs space, provokes molecules of all types to abandon their quiescence and allow themselves to be set into motion. A building is an illocutionary act (to yell "fire!" does not make a statement, it clears the room); it performs not only itself but a host of other possible worlds and scenarios that have waited invisibly, like units of embedded potential scattered through the world around it, only to be triggered or tapped. The "event" does not preexist the building, but it does wait silently, virtually, amid the precoherent rubble, to erupt, when ready, around it.

1. For a couple of days in February 1996 five of us converged in Ohio en groupuscule, assembled a traveling circus, engaged in a type of reunion at once premature and overdue. It was a reunion indeed, yet one with little concern for unity (a given that had never to date been spoken either) beyond the oddness of actually being there, together, amid the Ohio cornfields, and thus fulfilling in uncannily sudden fashion a destiny till then so hesitant in its unfolding that its progression could only be called glacial. Most of us — though not all — were there on official business to meet with Jay Chatterjee — to take in the new building at the University of Cincinnati, to write this book. Yet, on another register, we knew enough about what we ourselves might one day be in relation to one another to make us just a shade tense and tentative — we knew our paths met ineluctably down the way in a not-so-distant future, and the present meeting, though ostensibly about an important new building, felt something like a weird, if not unwelcome, trial run for something broader, something else. We had at least all been together in London at the Architectural Association with Alan (Jeff, Alejandro, Greg, me, and Ben, who that day, blissfully, came along for the ride), and knew that there was music somewhere among us, but that finding it would mean jamming . . . though selflessly and together. Egos. Egos already fouled but not yet damaged, but jealousy, compromise, petty greed, and misplaced ambition; could there be improvisatory research between us: was there a band here, or a carload of would-be-Elvises?

(Alan) Balfour, (Jeff) Kipnis, (Alejandro) Zaera-Polo, (Greg) Lynn, (Ben) van Berkel.

2. "If you want to make a historical impact, form a group and remain loyal to one another . . . no matter what." In another era the preceding prescription was still possible, and it seems, from today's standpoint, to have worked. History is nothing if not a savage process, and so its routines of predation must, at least somewhere and by certain operations, be kept at bay. Ideas are politics, politics war, and war fought with soldier-agents formed into higher aggregates: flexible squadrons, companies, and platoons. Old ideas, Gramsci showed us, don't die, they must be killed off. When new ideas replace them, they do so only as scarred victors, never as innate entitlements. Their tenures are reflections of their aptitudes, their capacities to resist recidivism or successive onslaughts. Ideas do not fight for themselves, but are anchored in the wills of those who struggle for them. Ideas are clearing, they make freedoms possible, but do not constitute freedom itself. Thus one's own freedom always depends on the unfettered freedom of another. Groups are political formations, all the more resilient when complex or heterogeneous; they are critical to the succession of ideas, to the production of historical novelty, to the elaboration of new freedoms and the unpredictable forms that follow from them. There is no single voice (monody) that is not in terrible danger of becoming despotic, fascist. The unchanging form of freedom is polyphony: multiple voices in linked unfolding.

Peter Eisenman, in conversation.

3. The excursion began with a much anticipated visit, not yet to a building but to an object — well, perhaps more than an object, if still not quite a building either: to the city of Columbus and Kipnis's Steinway B. Kipnis had been working his way through Schumann, Chopin, and Liszt, and I, interested in the Romantics as the ur-sprung of organicist philosophy, science, and aesthetics, forced a perennially delicate situation — successfully this time, to my astonishment — to get him to play some of this work for me on the new instrument (the grant of such audience has waited eight years). An impeccably black-lacquered Steinway is an awesome beast, but it is imperfect, inadequate in the most exquisite way: its magnificent sonority is simply that of piano mechanical structure (its keys, hammers, strings, pedals, and resonating board), not that of pure musical-becoming itself. This inbuilt tension between what can be notated, conceived, and, by strange, almost magical methods, induced in the mind-ear of the listener and what can actually be set into physical vibration through even the most brilliant deployment of given physical means has belonged at least to the semiconscious background of musical history since Bach's <u>Well-Tempered Klavier</u>. The idea that novelty (freedom) necessarily takes place <u>in the gap between</u> idea and realization and not within one of these poles themselves one might say is the foundation of the Romantic aesthetics and philosophy. As musicologist Charles Rosen put it, "The modern piano is [still] <u>sufficiently inadequate</u> to convey <u>Beethoven's intentions</u>." The primary point here is that a great deal of what properly belongs to "music" simply cannot, and could never, be embodied in physical "sound" per se, and yet this "extra" information is transmissible, albeit in inaudible ways. For the Romantics the transmission of inaudible structure had become a major project. In Schumann, for example, we find for the first time in history the presentation of the melodic line not by striking notes on the instrument, but by taking them away. These notes had previously been struck in a chord assembled of multiple voices, then rhythmically released from along the trajectory of their collective decay. Musical structure becomes a problem of exceedingly complex and subtle dynamics, the actual musical surface no longer carrying the greatest brunt of the informational burden. It has

ad libitum

Charles Rosen, <u>The Romantic Generation</u> (Cambridge: Harvard University Press, 1995), 3. Emphasis added.

Rosen, 10.

In other instances, notes which paradoxically were never sounded at all, are nonetheless notated to be released, or those which were in fact sounded are somehow released twice in a bizarre and spectral manner. Elsewhere in the Romantic canon, in Chopin for example, a perfectly homogeneous suite of ascending notes is somehow asked to express the inaudible passage from one measure to another.

become a surface in radically varied relief, with val-
leys that plunge into unfathomable mathematical
strife, a hypersensitive membrane meant to capture
even the faintest rumblings of multiple, distant logics
in interaction or collision. In my own mind, the soft,
confident wave-shape of Kipnis's piano is inseparable
from the massively abstract arguments that, in playing, and through the productive dynamics of structural default, the player makes it express.

4. It was the Aronoff Center for Design and Art that
brought us all to Ohio. Together. It would be ludicrous
to claim that any of us, in our own work, were toeing
a party line, that any of us harbored even the slightest
natural or strategic affinity for the Eisenmanian languages and shapes. And how many of us actually liked
the Center when we actually saw it? — it could hardly matter less. It was a work of fierce and undeniable
courage (on the part of the client as well as the architect). Courage. How many of us, I wonder, had what it
takes, and how many would still have it when things
got wild and rough? Courage to create not only one's
own work but to create the very possibility of architecture both for ourselves and for
everyone else? I myself doubt the
honesty of anyone who denies that
this is what Eisenman's work has
always been about. (Architects, an
articulate and generally wicked
bunch, speak endlessly ill of one
another, yet in 17 years I have
never once heard Eisenman
denounce a colleague, even if he did
cheer me on when I myself did so in
print.) There we were, a "new generation": no longer so young to be
diffident and merely of use; no
longer obscenely fresh, enthusiastic,
and innocently curious, but now
anxious, a little angry, aware of our
common ground, probably better
prepared than any generation
before us, and . . . well, almost
ready. I believed then and still do
now that it was part of the risk of
Eisenman's building to bring us to
Ohio, and we in turn spent there a
dangerous and productive two days.
Sure we will all write about

See Kipnis on
"something important"
page 170

Eisenman. We will admit tacitly that yes, in fact, his project did make us and ours possible, vastly expanding the concept and prestige of architectural <u>research</u>. And quite likely, in time, we will devour and obliterate most of the world he and his group created. But will we manage to carry the historical baton, will we continue to "build the possibility of building?" We all know, if only abstractly, that a stage is already being prepared for us somewhere, and during those days in Ohio the excitement (tempered by waves of distrust), was clearly palpable. Later on, (as the distrust dissipated) the more wild (from the point of view of history) things would become.

5. Among us, I was the only one who had previously written about the building. Five years ago, studying it through photographed models and drawings, I found it to be a building of undeniable significance. It mattered to me at the time that plastic, that is, material culture had begun to reflect fundamental changes in contemporary thinking, even from seemingly remote fields such as science and philosophy. I argued that it was one of the first postwar buildings based on thermodynamic principles that embodied real movement in a way few contemporary buildings had sought to do, and that since the time of the great midcentury organicists, it was among the first buildings to be given form in a fully active morphogenic space. Though I am not exactly a modernist (I still panic when the word arises in architectural discussions), I have always been totally committed to the necessity of <u>being</u> modern (as Rimbaud proposed) as a precondition to thinking the modern or what amounts to the same, to <u>thinking</u> actual becoming (though I am less certain of myself today). Regardless, no scientist aspires to do yesterday's science — of what use to reproduce Pasteur's or Lavoisier's results? — so why as designers would we aspire to recycle yesterday's realities? Worse, there is no middle ground: either fight one's way into the future or turn one's back on freedom, both one's own and, more significantly, the freedom of others. When this struggle with the future is carried out sincerely, and in the Aronoff Center I believe it is, one must ask whether the present is fully entitled to judge it at all. Little matter, for it would never stop anyone. But my point is not to disparage the present, rather to question the complacency with which we make judgments (to disqualify speculation has become an all too common pastime of both the right and the correct left). On

Peter Eisenman, Lecture at Rice University, February 1996.

The specter of an upcoming exhibition of some prominence, in our control and of our own making, had already begun to flush out the first residues of grabbing and naive ambition.

"The Genius of Matter: Eisenman's Cincinnati Project," in Peter Eisenman & Frank Gehry (New York: Rizzoli International, 1991).

this question, there was complete consensus among us. Since 1991, each of us has gone on to develop work within the framework that this building, at least in my admittedly strange rendition of it, proposed. I have no doubt, indeed I have felt this since late 1989, that something new has been emerging in design circles of very general and fundamental import; not just a novel set of shapes and forms, but a new type of rationality and a new intuition of space as an active medium, shaped not by tools but by adjacent, embedded, and remote events and the routines and logics they trigger. The Aronoff Center has served, in no small way I believe, as a marker for all of us who have been struggling to give conceptual and plastic expression to this new order of things. We five scarcely discussed the building's particulars during those days in Ohio, and yet, from the viewpoint of the future whose forces have already clearly and palpably begun to press, our trip from the outset had taken on the retroactive flavor of a collective pilgrimage.

6. Does Eisenman understand or really care about the things of which we think and talk? It would at most be safe to say that he listens, though not carefully, that he is watchful, yet not particularly engaged. Eisenman after all is a structuralist, and oppositional logic is at bottom what he is truly attentive to. This mindset has little to do with our mode of working (it is rather the nightmare from which we strive, and have already with some success begun, to awaken), and yet . . . we were there. The cynical will say that it is simply in Eisenman's interest to cycle his work through the mind and laboratories of a new generation of practitioners, but Eisenman has never wanted for youthfulness (rather the opposite). Besides, the work often stands up to vigorous encounters with new ideas; the same cannot be said for the work of his contemporaries. Eisenman's embrace of the computer, though not notably sophisticated unless one considers the way in which it repeats John Cage's use of the I Ching, has been the focus of his latest gambit attempting to transfer deterministic control away from a putative monophonic human intentionality. The computer in such a deployment is supposed to provide a disinterested inflectionary voice that forces continual collaboration and improvisation with other, "human-all-too-human" players. Eisenman remains entirely fixed on overcoming what the 1970s called "humanism," but like many others of his generation he has not fully

See Barry on "the realization of this building" page 49

noticed that the most successful gestures in this direction rarely issued from such willful, self-conscious acts, or that the dead "author" that was once so gleefully embraced by theorists ever lived a life quite as impoverished as the one their philosophy imagined for it. (The recent switch of emphasis toward discourses of Life and to the density of independent relations and processes that issue from the polyphonic human substrate — the Body — have by now rendered such homicidal posturing parochial at best.) Now, it is a curious — though not altogether comprehensible — common desire today to seek to generate so-called Piranesian effects in one's architecture. The Piranesi-effect Eisenman seeks is specifically the effect of unforeseeable complexity that arises from multiple interfering structures blindly pursuing their own clockwork logic. Dissonance clearly plays a critical role here, indeed to some eyes it serves (though mistakenly in my opinion) as the very sign that such complexity has been achieved. The Aronoff Center is nothing if not a tour de force of this kind. I have never had the experience of such a building before: every step and every cavity seems interstitial, transitional, willfully channeling on the way to somewhere else. The pathways that I showed in my 1991 article as the "cyclic flow of instability" in the field or macrostructure actually appear in the realized building indiscriminately everywhere, that is, at the micro- and

See Kolbowski on "no hierarchy of good, better, and best" page 136

x=382.41
y=159.46
z=785.50

Go to 400 Level NE Plan page 80

meso- scales as well. But clearly "we" five share a different concept of complexity than the one Eisenman is using, a different order of desired effects. For us dissonance is actually but a case of remote, even hyper-remote, <u>consonance</u> (we seek to move away from the clockwork model of propagation and distribution toward a nonlinear, algorithmic, or living one). Consonance for us is not reactionary quite simply

Go to
500 Level NC Plan
page 87

See Hays on
"extreme chromaticism"
page 26

x = 222.89
y = 186.47
z = 801.00

because it is "soft," that is, because it belongs to a mobile universe in which its role is to transmit regulatory pressures, to orient vaguely, not to assign rigid positions or relations. Arnold Schoenberg's atonal system had these affects already built into it, and it released an entirely new spectrum of material sonority that has never had need of the simple-minded stochastics that dictate much artificially agitated architectural production today. After Schoenberg, no sonority was ever understood to be stable, simple, or monophonic. Even a single tone possessed a plurality that was inexhaustible and irreducible to a single dimension or relation. At the heart of every event there is coloration and periodicity.

7. Standing outside the building, tracing the slow, restrained heave of its S-curves on two axes, it is Kipnis's <u>piano</u> that comes back to mind. (As everyone always forgets, piano means nothing other than soft.) The piano is of course a soft system, but that is primarily due to the way it opens itself to the infinite, often extreme manipulations of composer and player. A soft system refers to the aspect of any coherent ensemble that ensures its continuing coherence or stability over a broad range of conditions or changing values. In other words, the perceivable structure is tethered to mobile or flexible parameters that are buried or distributed in the system. These produce the effect of <u>regulation</u>; they act like guides ensuring that every development in a suite of processes surfs information generated from the system's earlier states. The sum effect is that the whole remains in interaction with itself, with its parts, and with all of its past, future, and possible states. Through resonance and periodicity comes a kind of material <u>intelligence</u>. There is a marvelous tradition in music beginning with, for example, Schumann, who, in his early <u>Humoresk</u>, writes a meso- or inter-voice for the piano that slips between the bass and the treble lines, a voice, however, that is not played, but is meant to link

and interface the two other hands in some higher dimensional manifold. This eccentric but continuous tradition passes through to late-20th-century works such as those of Ligeti, certain schools of jazz, improvisation, and dub reggae where entire tracks or notes are physically or electronically deleted from the works' finished versions, which continue nonetheless to leave remote structural shadows of their once-embedded but now entirely distributed and therefore invisible influence. The player-piano approach of an Eisenman, who in 1960s conceptualist fashion is content to generate, at as great a remove as possible, a set of events unfurled from a rigorous but fixed logic and then to feed these into the system for a direct, mechanical readout, moves in a direction very different from what I will call the "organicist" models cited above. The organicists always work within a conception of multiplicity which is active, variable, temporally oriented, and transactional rather than deterministic. To reach what he calls the "unforeseeable," Eisenman constructs systems of interweaving logic, but only in order to submit passively to the arbitrary and the serendipitous; the organicists seek to achieve this effect (the "undetermined") by tapping into these systems as engines or reservoirs of coherent fluid potential. In the end it is a question of noise versus information, integration, and resonance.

These compositional techniques have been a constant source of inspiration for Bruce Mau and me in our work at ZONE. See my "Two dimensional Design as an n-Dimensional Problem," in Michael Bell and Tse-Tsung Leong eds., Slow Space, forthcoming with The Monacelli Press, 1997.

8. At the heart of every event, I wrote above, there is coloration and periodicity. It is, I hope, no longer farfetched or even particularly tendentious to claim that architecture is a specific type of deployment of patterned events. No biologist would refuse this definition of living architecture, and no composer or musician would refuse this as an interpretation of musical structure. In all of these milieus complexity and novelty are products of the interplay between different rates of repeated events. Every flow structure is either itself periodic (its "order" need not be directly visible or audible and may be lodged at extremely remote points in time or space) or else draws from a multidimensional substrate of interacting periodic structures. Almost all architectures have an explicit base periodicity — tantamount to a percussion section in a musical ensemble — and if they do not, their very singularity may be said to issue from that fact (rhetorically obliterating this grounding, centralizing periodicity is today becoming an increasingly common parti in architectural production.) Amid the entire moving mass of forms and events that make up a building there may almost always be discerned a fundamental "voice" that provides punctuation, keeps time, and distributes what might be called metrical intensities and rhythmic potential. One need think no farther than the simple distribution of alternating bays (a/b/a) in a classical (and/or modernist) villa. Now, the free jazz experiments of the 1960s and '70s effected a greater and greater emancipation of drumwork from the anchoring and timekeeping role, giving way to the remarkable new spaces of polymetric and unmetric unfoldings; today a number of designers have begun to explore these new spaces in 2- and 3-D plastic composition. Yet a single glance from almost any point inside the Aronoff Center — regardless of what one knows to be true of the system of rationality that generated it — produces an undeniable effect of near-unmeter. This, in a phrase, is the highly sought Piranesi-effect. For many, however, the road must go farther.

9. Can one go beyond Piranesi? The indisputable answer is yes. Consider the modern percussionist. Every limb of the drummer oscillates at an independent and different rate. Some oscillations include "partials" that fit easily into some clear "fundamental" value, but whether they do this or not, the varied oscillations are all, in some strict mathematical manner, related. Today, the fundamental itself is almost never audibly present in the composition, nor for that matter is it necessary. But it does exist, for in the final analysis every percussionist draws on the fundamental oscillator of the breath (according to many traditions this oscillator connects the body's oscillator to all other ones in the universe, astronomical and molecular). As the performing body begins to sustain multiple standing waves, the heartbeat and, more locally, the pulses may be tapped into either to syncopate or underwrite departures from the dominant structural line. To modify these oscillators, to multiply their number, for example, would undermine the dominance and centrality of the major line. For a long time this was thought — at least in music — to be nearly impossible, indeed impossible on purely neurological grounds. Then came experimentalists such as Milford Graves who sought to liberate themselves from the tyranny of rigid, monodic musical time. Graves's legendary status as one of the greatest percussionists of all time relies primarily on one remarkable feat: his

See Forster on "a virtually Piranesian feat" page 119

capacity to vary the strength of the coupling of his body's internal oscillators as generators of rhythmic patterns. Graves is able to control his heartbeat at will (speeding it up and slowing it down to a near stand-still) and to vary the pulse in each of his limbs inde-pendently of the rate of his heart. The free, or true, nonmetrical drumming issuing from Graves's single organism throws a humbling challenge to the arid, mechanical performances of millenarian posthuman-ist rhetoric in architecture and the other arts. In Milford Graves the substrate (or fundamental) oscilla-tor is itself no longer fixed as ground but totally mobile and massively distributed: the performing sub-ject both proliferates and effectively vanishes into the full density and plenitude of matter, into a manifold of continuously variable times (periodicities). It remains controversial in music circles whether true polymeter really exists or whether it is an elaborate but insoluble illusion.

Even for Schoenberg the question whether dissonance was real and absolute or merely the illusionary per-spectival effect of having invented a new distance from correlated oscillators remains unresolved. Now the answer to this question, however, is unimportant: what matters is what new types of consistency can be invent-ed to hold a composition together as a series of synco-pated expressive events, not whether its formal logic can be rent asunder in the name of a crude, destructive radicality, unmooring its elements and condemning them to aphasia, miscellaneity, and the wages of entropy. The fifteen minutes of architecture's decon-structivist glory in 1988 is a good, recent example of misguided, 20th-century pseudo-antirationalism (though to be fair, few of its practitioners were as com-pletely duped as its theorists). In great part it is the naiveté and the one-dimensionality of this so-called rad-ical tradition that the emerging generation must vigor-ously reject. What we seek is no different from what most of genuine modern radical thought and practice has sought: to force every apparent natural unity to yield and to express the coursing multiplicities of which it is made. In other words, it is always to find the "ensemble" pulsing wildly at the heart of every solo.

10. For Eisenman the Aronoff Center represents in many ways Moses's Pisgah sight of Palestine. In rela-tion to Eisenman's oeuvre, the building belongs to what in traditional art historical circles is sometimes called the "late style." The late style is a complex phe-

See his Harmonielehre.

Moses brought the Israelites through the desert for forty years but was not permitted to enter the promised land with them. In his last days, he climbed Mount Pisgah and surveyed the Land of Israel from afar.

nomenon: it is characterized both by a sudden fresh-
ness that seems to come from nowhere, and a clarity
and singleness that approaches true indifference to the
doubts that mined the career that preceded it (this is
not always good). In Eisenman's case it is not a new
clarity and the absence of layered doubt that can be
seen to emerge here (all of his work depends on a thick
sediment of strife), but what may well represent the
closest he may ever come to embracing the real duration that inhabits the interstitial realm from which
form and matter arise. In other words, it constitutes
what may be his only encounter with real, rather than
purely rhetorical, space. But even this can be truly
deduced only from the diagram that the Aronoff
Center projects into the world, not in the many details
of its material realization. It remains a concrete diagram of acutely focused intellectual and mechanical
processes, perversely proud of its detachment from the
chaotic, wet realities of the nonlinear world, those
very realities that are of central interest to our project
today. The age of the player piano is over; the age of
free, disciplined, and organic improvisation has perhaps only begun, but the Aronoff Center provides an
important bridge between the two. The intensities that
musical improvisation seeks to release can be made to
appear only against a ground of weaving, repeating,
and interfering structures, but these structures must
be sensitive, sentient, in communication with one
another, part of a system in continual dynamic integration. Every fact of nature can be seen as such an
organism, whole and self-repairing or, to put it another way, as oriented. This does not mean that stochastics (Xenakis) or total serialism (Boulez) are necessarily dead ends, only that the search for new integrative
intensities have, in these cases, been pushed to different levels and with different parameters of constraints.
Eisenmanian total serialism (a compositional process
in which musical events are distributed according to
rigid mathematical determinations) has in the Aronoff
Center finally given way — if only just a little — to the
same type of glissandi that, in the notorious Phillips
Pavilion, Yannis Xenakis once felicitously introduced
into Le Corbusier's flatfooted planimetric scheme. The
task for the five of us, and for our like-minded friends,
will be to make of the Aronoff Center our own perverse and unwilling precursor.

A compositional process according to which musical events are
distributed according to very rigid mathematical determinations.

See Zaera-Polo on
"a machinic performance"
page 29

Sanford Kwinter is
director of the Institute
for Design Research at
Rensselaer Polytechnic
Institute, New York.

x=112.12
y=80.30
z=820.00

Go to
600 Level NW Plan
page 92

x=93.42
y=67.15
z=820.60

Go to
600 Level NW Plan
page 92

600 Level

Library stair to stacks

The Aronoff Center contains 91,000 square feet of studio, lab, and office space.

x=160.65
y=42.54
z=816.50

Go to
600 Level NW Plan
page 93

600 Level

x=208.80
y=109.65
z=818.17

Go to
600 Level NW Plan
page 93

600 Level

P-TR'S PROGRESS

Jeffrey Kipnis

PROLOGUE
**Theory helps those of us who do practical work to determine the direction, to see the future clearly, to be resolute in action and to have confidence in the success of our work.
Joseph Stalin**

**Night and day I dream of having my actions recorded in history. The most dishonorable way to win a name for oneself is through scholarly compositions, but at the moment it is the only way I know . . .
Ho Chi Minh**

Whatever its merits as a work of architecture, the Aronoff Center for Design and Art confirms Eisenman's talent in another crucial area of the discipline, the construction of a professional persona. He has cultivated an Elmer Gantry character that enables him to persuade his clients to invest in nothing more than, but nothing less than, form. "But that is architecture!" he intones.

The genius of Eisenman's professional craft lies not only in his abilities to convince his clients of his difficult designs, but also in his will to guide them — the designs and the clients — through the protracted dissonance they encounter on their way to realization. Many, when they first confront the Aronoff Center, will quip that it is amazing that the architect gets such things built. Few will realize that they have said something important.

Eisenman honed his professional skills in the classrooms of Princeton, Harvard, The Cooper Union, and elsewhere. Always controversial, he nevertheless emerged as one of a generation's legendary teachers. In each class he could be heard to declare, "But that is architecture," as he urged students into an obedient awe of form.

"But that is architecture." Even today, Eisenman continues to mesmerize all comers with that passionate trope — so effective because it forecloses dissent even as it claims to deepen discussion. It is not difficult to imagine why few of his students rarely found a way to the measured reply, "No, architecture is more than form."

1. PHENOMENAL TRANSPARENCY

Of course, long before he took to the lectern, Eisenman had himself been inducted into the formalist creed by Colin Rowe. In passing and on the way to outlining a deeply conservative position, Rowe opened the door to a post-Wölfflinian formalism that, despite his best efforts, he could not hold in check. "The Mathematics of the Ideal Villa," "Literal and Phenomenal Transparency" (with Robert Slutzky), and his precocious attention to certain Modern Masters (Le Corbusier, Terragni) — albeit a perverse attention bent on subsuming these architects into his antiprogressivist project — earned for Rowe the bizarre status of the intellectual progenitor of the American avant-garde.

In the two mentioned essays, Rowe employed clever gimmicks to make his formalist case persuasive. Consider, for example, the hyperbolic titles. Given that architects are congenitally terrified that their art is merely superficial, who among them could resist Rowe's ponderous promises of profundity. No matter that the "Mathematics of the Ideal Villa" turned out to be a couple of cubes on grass or that "Phenomenal Transparency" ended up nothing more than a catchy bon mot for an interesting formal effect. The titles were their own guarantors, their own source of depth.

See Hays on "ur-theorist Colin Rowe" page 22

x=378.59
y=234.38
z=812.73

Go to 500 Level NE Reflected Ceiling Plan page 84

But Rowe's best trick was his canny use of examples. To ensure that the then-fashion for glass, lamentable to his retrograde tastes, fell short of more traditional solid materials, he pitted a modest Gropius against a Corbusian tour de force, remaining silent about Mies's considerably more convincing uses of glass. To indemnify his an-historical formal comparisons in "Mathematics," he invoked two masterworks, each of consummate quality in its use of material, construction, detail, program, light and shadow, siting, space, etc., allowing the issue of form to be artificially foregrounded.

The technique was simple but effective sophistry: twist the fact that great architecture often has intricate formal properties into an argument that intricate formal properties constitute great architecture. Most understood the distortion as rhetorical device; even if they followed Rowe's emphasis on form, they kept on eye on the balance of their architectural palette. Though Eisenman, a formidable critic early on, no doubt recognized the device as well, he embraced formalism with apostolic fervor.

Yet, let us not assume that Eisenman's ecstatic tunnel vision doomed his architecture de jure. Though it has shackled his work with limitations, limitations that reach a critical point at the Aronoff Center, it has also allowed him to produce architectural effects never before imagined. These, too, reach a frenzied peak in Cincinnati, a peek at the brink of madness.

Virtually all of Eisenman's inventions derive from the Rowe/Slutzky treatment of Phenomenal Transparency. Despite the authors' effort to edify their terminology with dictionary quotations, their use of the term <u>phenomenal</u> is nonsensical, notwithstanding its remarkable cachet. Nevertheless, Phenomenal Transparency has become the proper name for an important formal effect: the use of formal relations to express on opaque facades the increasingly complex sections made possible by modern construction. The transparency thus achieved is conceptual. It is not seen, but read; it belongs not to the senses, but to the mind.

It is doubtful that Le Corbusier sought to achieve the particular effect as described by Rowe and Slutzky; its availability at Garche is more likely an artifact of the architect's general bent for coherence. No matter; the authors' convincing account of the effect gave birth to its possibility as an explicit project. With their analysis, the authors introduced a new stage in the textualization of architectural form and gave momentum to the transformation of contemporary architecture from the sensual to the intellectual, a transformation that mirrored processes well underway in the other arts.

2. PHENOMENAL TRANSLUCENCY

The Rowe/Slutzky argument transfixed Eisenman. According to the architect's own account, his preoccupation with their expanded textual-

---

Unlike Rowe's argument for formal typology in "Mathematics," which Eisenman virtually ignored. That essay argues the persistent viability of a limited catalogue of formal types across history, providing the linchpin for Rowe's conservative attack on zeitgeist theories. It was, therefore, anathema to Eisenman's avant-gardist ambitions.

Strictly speaking, what Rowe and Slutzky name "literal transparency" is a phenomenal effect, and their "phenomenal transparency" is an interpretive, and therefore literary, effect. Yet, despite possible appearances, I do not offer this observation as pedantry; to the contrary, I admire and subscribe to the authors' preference for rhetorical effect over scholarly rigor. I am particularly grateful to them for the term in question, whose (eisen) manic transformations structure this essay.

Eisenman recognized both the persuasive power of typological arguments and their threat to his position. He initially attempted to outflank typological theory with a deep structure argument for architectural form, following Noam Chomsky. The benefits of such a formulation to Eisenman's project are still apparent. 1. It would reinforce the configuration of architecture as a textual (intellectual) system. 2. It would allow for persistent formal types, analogous to specific languages, without making these the foundation of architectural knowledge, much as Chomsky's work accounted for particular languages without making any specific language or ur-language the basis of linguistic theory. 3. Finally and most importantly, it would emphasize the open-endedness of design. Chomsky had already shown that an infinite number of statements, most of which would be new, were enabled by the finite number of rules of his generative grammar.

However promising this approach was, it quickly proved intractable for the architect. He soon settled for appropriating formal types into his manipulations by reducing them to signs. While this approach allowed him to acknowledge typology without obligating his architecture to its restrictive regimens, it ultimately skirted the key conservative claim that all received formal types embody persistent patterns of use and meaning, and that all persistent patterns of use and meaning have already engendered formal types. Eisenman's failure to confront the typology issue head-on has left his work vulnerable to the criticism, particularly from the old-left, that it constitutes mere indulgence in fashion, rather than an authentic avant-garde.

ization of formal relations was immediate and powerful. He saw in it the possibility of fulfilling architecture's long-lived, but long deferred ambition to achieve full status as a critical cultural apparatus. With such sophisticated formal effects, he argued, architects would be able to write cultural commentary in architecture.

For years, Eisenman meticulously cultivated the Phenomenal Transparency effect into an entire repertoire of formal devices. As he proceeded through his 12 houses (I–X, El Even Odd, Fin D'Out Hous) and through such projects as the Cannaregio Housing and Wexner Center, he slowly mastered the technique of using process to coordinate ensembles of formal effects into increasingly ambitious and complex texts. In these designs, whether the textual subject matter was discursive or fictional, the architect remained faithful to the premise of a legible perspicacity of formal relationships fundamental to the original Rowe/Slutzky notion.

With those early works, Eisenman also went out of his way to broadcast his unconditional commitment to formal relationships over all other architectural values. He exalted in ignoring material traditions, using any expedient material as long as it allowed him to construct, and afford to construct, his forms. He systematically choreographed his form-texts to encroach on function. Whenever he published a project he included a complete exposition of the formal processes; if the publication was of a building, he chose photographs that confirmed the formal achievements. No images of people enjoying their homes, no pleasant views, no atmospheric interiors. Just Form.

At some point, beginning perhaps with the Romeo and Juliet project

and certainly in full flower by the La Villette garden, a transformation occurred: Eisenman began to elaborate the formal intricacy of his designs well beyond the point of legibility. While he maintained an unfailing rigor in his deployment and annotation of formal relationships in these projects — thus preserving, in principle at least, the possibility of a correct reading — the sheer number of devices, repeated at several

An entire repertoire
of formal devices

x=280.77
y=100.65
z=801.00

Go to
500 Level NC Plan
page 87

scales, and an increasing tendency to compel these devices to intersect and superpose, made legibility a practical impossibility.

In Eisenman's hands, the effect so cherished by Rowe, that is, the directed transmission of interior formal relations through the facade and by way of the eye to the mind of a discerning subject, gave way to mind-boggling spectra of formal reflections, refractions, and diffractions no longer obeying any simple sense of origin or directionality. Dazzling disarray supplanted tasteful clarity as the architect entangled his viewer in a web of the formal counterparts to mirrors and veils, driving beyond Phenomenal Transparency to an entirely new architectural effect: Phenomenal Translucency.

3. PHEROMONAL TRANSLUCENCY

This new music frustrates me. . . .
Its composers seem to think rather than feel.
Sergei Rachmaninov

The point of critique is not justification but a
different way of feeling, another sensibility.
Gilles Deleuze

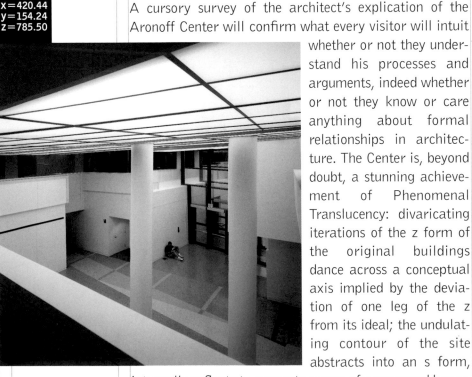

x=420.44
y=154.24
z=785.50

Go to
400 Level NE Plan
page 80

A cursory survey of the architect's explication of the Aronoff Center will confirm what every visitor will intuit whether or not they understand his processes and arguments, indeed whether or not they know or care anything about formal relationships in architecture. The Center is, beyond doubt, a stunning achievement of Phenomenal Translucency: divaricating iterations of the z form of the original buildings dance across a conceptual axis implied by the deviation of one leg of the z from its ideal; the undulating contour of the site abstracts into an s form, internally reflects to generate a rope of superposed boxes, and then hangs like a necklace on the z group so that the two organizational systems (z & s) and the box elements of each blur into one another to create a fabulous, bewildering spectacle. However intriguing one may find the mechanisms of the design — its processes and notations — these offer nothing to account for the building's visceral impact.

The Center is everywhere discomforting, and it is no accident that once you are inside it, the sensation it most elicits is that of being immersed in the mis-en-abyme of reflections in an immense, mirrored room. But it is the on the exterior where the darkest consequences of the transition from Phenomenal Transparency to Phenomenal Translucency first erupt.

The sequence of facades grips you with a fulsome ambivalence; as you move around the building, you experience incessant waves of fascination and dread. You confront a badly dissected harlequin splayed open to reveal alien organs, piebald and swollen. Unable to take your eyes off the macabre scene, you discover the xeno-vitals to be but real organs transected and recombined like a delirious fugue. You realize your first intuition was wrong. Far from being the result of incompetence, it is an expert work by a master surgeon, one driven to operate at the limit of technique but wearied of the traditions and values of his art. When you leave it, the building clings to you, not as a memory, but as an odor, partly erotic, partly necrotic.

An obtuse description, no doubt. But one that speaks to a crucial change of register magnified by the Center's perfection of Phenomenal Translucency. Even as the design of the building claims to be a conceptual enterprise, its unfathomable complexity silently underwrites a certain reaffirmation of sensation over intellection. Eisenman had discovered early on that some of the most interesting aspects of his buildings were the unexpected experiences they produced, such as the giant, layered perspectival tubes generated by the grid-lattice of the Wexner Center. As sensations rather than understandings, these unintended effects did not properly belong to the formal readings the architect set out to embody.

Yet neither could they be simply detached from those readings; the latter established the receptive field, the milieu of sensibility for the new experiences. The Wexner's perspectival tunnels, for example, would not

See Kolbowski on "not without its discomforts" page 137

have felt the same, perhaps would not even have been noticed, had the lattice appeared at the Wexner Center as a traditional architectural figure, e.g., a trellised pergola, rather than as but a moment in an elaborate scheme of grid notations suffusing the whole building and its site. Directed toward reading, toward interpretation, most of those notations were experientially flat. Thus, the encounter with the perspectival tunnels offered a particular shock.

See Hays on "critical representations" page 23

At first Eisenman treated these experiential aspects of his designs as just dessert, as interest earned on a cerebral investment in the design process. But as the designs grew more complex and the possibility of reading receded, these effects gained increased importance, overtaking the status of interpretation. Formal textuality and process stopped being ends in themselves and became the techniques by which unusual sensibilities were achieved. Once desperate to leave behind the pre-critical realm of architectural sensibilities in order to achieve a critical architecture, Eisenman now steered a post-critical turn toward new sensibilities, new feelings.

"**pher-o-mone** (fêr´•ə•mōn), n. 1. <u>Animal Behav</u>. Any chemical substance released by an animal that serves to influence the sexual behavior of another member of the same species. 2. Chemicals whose <u>physical form induces changes in behavior or affect in animals and are able to act at remote distances from the source</u>. [1959. Gk.]" [emphasis added]

Eisenman's theoretical treatment of affect derives somewhat circuitously from Freud, who used the term to accent the mobility of expressed emotions and their independence from expressed representations. For example, in a dream one may report seeing a pleasant scene but experiencing an inappropriate feeling such as fear. In this case, an affect had moved from its original source and attached to the pastoral representation.

To distinguish post-critical from pre-critical sensibilities and to call attention to the fact that the emotional impact of the work emanates not from the representations of the architecture but from the formal structures themselves, Eisenman termed these new sensations collectively as "affects." Thus, while the original objective of Eisenman's architecture was reading, its ultimate objective became affect. And the Aronoff Center is nothing if not a seething cauldron of affects.

As the consummation of this change of objective, the Center also completes Eisenman's two-decade long reconstruction of Rowe's ideal modern subject, the patient, reflective connoisseur, into a contemporary subject who is never quite ideal, who, perpetually agitated and buffeted by irrepressible appetites, cannot simply see or read, but watches, gawks, gazes, and stares, a schizo-voyeur. The Center is a limit condition, an extreme case. Not merely Phenomenal Translucency, then, but something more promiscuous. Pheromonal Translucency?

Or, given the rupture wrought by the Viconian return of Eisenman's architecture to feelings and sensibilities, a return driven not by retreating from arcane form, but by driving form beyond the arcane, by driving form crazy, perhaps the Center is best considered a case of —

4. PHEROMONAL TRANSLUNACY

See Whiting on
"redirects the subject's glance"
page 98

**The best thing about Peter's buildings is the insane spaces he ends up with. That's why he is an important architect. All that other stuff, the philosophy and all, is just bullshit as far as I'm concerned.
Frank Gehry**

Eisenman's plunge into an architecture of post-critical sensibilities brings into focus certain chronic limitations of his technique. The most conspicuous at the Center is the inadequacy of his formal procedures to conceptualize and deploy materials in roles richer than providing shape and notation. This despite the fact that, with the exception of light and shadow, perhaps no other aspect of a building is so saturated with affective expectation.

Without doubt, architects have made the best use of material effects in building and provided the most articulate and colorful meditations on them — consider, for example, Louis Kahn's conversation with a brick. Nevertheless, the materiality of buildings is by no means a topic exclusive to architecture. The fundamental insinuation of material affectivity across many cultures has long been in evidence well beyond the boundaries of architecture, in art, literature, mythology, and elsewhere. Even the three little pigs and the wolf knew of it.

Go to
wall section
page 122

At the onset of his design career Eisenman used his radical formalism as an opportunity to neuter architecture's venerated tradition of evocative materiality, which he saw as irremediably sentimental and therefore pre-critical. As a result, all of his works to date are built in non-emotive materials used strictly to make forms and to code formal relations, that is, to support the textuality of the design. In the early projects in particular, materiality, albeit under erasure, was intrinsic to the architect's theoretical position.

As affect became increasingly important in his work, however, Eisenman's position on materiality quietly slipped from the purely theoretical. By the time he is building the Aronoff Center, the architect, aware of the affective potential of materiality, attempts belatedly to recapture it for his project. The finishing material for the exterior, for example, was originally a far more convincing Italian tile.

The Center, however, was designed strictly as a formal exercise; material considerations entered the design only as a desirable appurtenance, a rendering tool without any necessary, intrinsic relationship to the project's conception. Thus, when financial considerations imposed the inevitable Sophie's Choice between materials and form, Eisenman had no convincing alternative but to sacrifice materials.

x=310.74
y=218.66
z=801.00

Go to
500 Level NC Plan
page 87

Go to
facade
page 76

Had the architect not broached the question of affect, his material technique may never have posed a serious problem. But with the onset of his move toward post-critical sensibilities, it is proving a handicap — in part because of lost affective opportunity, in part because his material choices undermine the potential power of his forms. At the Center, the consequences are most acutely evident on the exterior.

The facades of the Center are rendered in pigmented EIFS, a synthetic stucco that is the architectural equivalent to food coloring and gruel. Nontectonic and void of any intrinsic qualities, this faux-material and others like it are often chosen today for large, difficult forms because they are inexpensive, highly plastic, and easy to use. As such, they are typically found in the construction of pseudo-historical buildings, theme parks, and miniature golf courses. Like theater sets, however, these constructions need only suspend disbelief, an effect dependent on the generous receptivity of an audience. To achieve its full potential as a work of architecture, a building must not depend on generosity. It must surpass the suspension of disbelief, insisting itself on all constituencies by looking and feeling, by being real.

As other contemporary architects have discovered, materials need not be traditional, precious, or valorized to meet a standard of insistence. But the facades of the Center are less than materially insistent and suffer the repercussions. Many persons, for example, have found fault with Eisenman's choice of exterior colors. The colors are indeed jarring, but, on the other hand, they contribute substantially to the disturbing effect. It is not the colors per se, but the use of irresolute materials that causes those colors to be less than convincing and tacitly licenses grousing.

Whatever weaknesses the Aronoff Center suffers in materiality are more than overshadowed by the success of its exotic interior spaces. Circulating through the halls and rooms, one is overwhelmed by a masterpiece of Eisenman's interior style: staggered and shifting streams of pastel elements — columns, beams, walls — merge into and emerge from one another, intriguing windows puncture walls according to an order other than the traditional relationship to light or views, and so forth. To this signature palette the Center contributes a braided organization that snakes in plan and section like a giant caduceus, abandoned and on the verge of going feral.

It is important to note that the "material reality" of a building is not a natural outgrowth of some unchanging phenomenological essence of particular materials — wood, stone, steel — but an architectural effect whose persuasiveness, like any special effect, is open to the vicissitudes of changing contexts, attitudes, and techniques. Along this line, it is interesting to observe how some materials, e.g., marble or teak, once revered in architecture and revisited in the last decade by some architects, are today so extravagant that their use in a building renders it farcically irreal. Cf. London's Canary Wharf.

See Cobb on "gypsum wallboard" page 97

Go to
corridor
page 182

As one moves through the building, again and again one comes upon astonishing spaces, moments in the building where all of its modes of interest — its elaborate formal relationships, its displacing affects, its twining plan and layered section, even its neutered materiality — converge and coalesce into an operatic chorus whose swells of assonance and dissonance are more transporting than any of its individual voices. While these dramatic moments occur in the primary voids of the building, e.g., the central triple-height atrium and the main theater, they are also found at less conspicuous locales, such as the entry to the building from the campus parking lot and the umbilical foyer that joins the navels of the old and new buildings.

The network of hyperactive spaces at the Center are far superior to those achieved in Eisenman's previous built works and more convincingly linked throughout the building by the connective tissue of his stylistic palette. As a whole, the interiors absorb and agitate and push the visitor to multiple edges: to the edge of vertigo, to the edge of confusion, to the edge of credibility.

The interiors alone assure that the Center will assume the status of the finest of Eisenman's works to date. Indeed, it is difficult to imagine that the architect could possibly squeeze any more surprises out of his textual-formal techniques. Hence, one suspects that, wherever the architect takes design from here, the Center will also stand as the culminating achievement of this line of his inquiry.

The Aronoff Center, however, is not just a work within Eisenman's ouevre; it is one of the crowning achievements of a period of architectural research, taking its place alongside such buildings as Daniel Libeskind's Jewish Museum in Berlin and Frank Gehry's Guggenheim Museum in Bilbao. For the last two decades, these architects and others have concentrated their various efforts on an architecture of radical singularity, that is, the design of buildings that neither follow any other building as a prototype nor offer themselves as new prototypes.

This eschewal of prototypical ambition has its roots in a reaction against the stultifying Corporate Modernism enabled, if not authorized, by the explicitly prototypical researches of the early modernists. This prototypical intent continues in full force today in the work of the neo-historicists and certain new modernists. Over time, however, the architecture of radical singularity has tried to outgrow its initial formulation as a mere refusal and/or rejection of dominant architectural principles. Architects and theorists have been attempting to formulate an alternative body of ideas intended to construct radical singularity as a positive social, cultural, and political project for architecture, that is, as a continuously viable mode of practice.

As is to be expected, radical singularity has met with the same predictable uneasiness from the public as all other new and unusual ideas, though it has earned wide attention in academic circles. However admirable the motives of these architects, however extraordinary their results, with only a relatively few exemplary buildings to assess, it is far too early to determine the larger significance of this model of architectural practice. It may well be that

Go to
500 Level NC Plan
page 87

x=280.05
y=133.63
z=801.00

See Zaera-Polo on
"the criteria to assess"
page 37

radical singularity will cast a permanent pall on prototypical practices, or it may be that its avoidance of prototypical research may ultimately prove a dereliction. In retrospect, the Aronoff Center may be seen as a pivotal work in a new era of architecture or a climactic work of a fascinating period consigned to the irrelevant because it broached no enduring influence.

Whatever its ultimate impact on the future of architecture, there can be no doubt that the Aronoff Center will enjoy a well-deserved period of study and attention. Outrageous scion of a coupling between a house of cards and a hall of mirrors, the Center is fun house become work of art. No small achievement.

Jeffrey Kipnis is professor of architecture at Ohio State University in Columbus, Ohio, and a critic. Most recently he was director of graduate studies at the Architectural Association in London.

x=389.36
y=157.77
z=813.63

Go to
500 Level NE Reflected Ceiling Plan
page 84

ARONOFF CENTER
FOR DESIGN AND ART

COLLEGE OF DESIGN,
ARCHITECTURE,
ART, AND PLANNING

UNIVERSITY OF
CINCINNATI

CLIENT
University of Cincinnati

PRESIDENT
Joseph A. Steger

VICE PRESIDENT FOR FINANCE
Dale L. McGirr

DEAN
Jay Chatterjee

UNIVERSITY ARCHITECT
Ronald B. Kull
James Alexander Jr., John Childress,
Jeffrey Johnson, Kristi Nelson,
Raymond Renner, Joseph Power,
Nicholaus Scheper, Barry Stedman,
Robert Yaun

ARCHITECT
Eisenman Architects

PRINCIPAL-IN-CHARGE
Peter Eisenman, FAIA

ASSOCIATES-IN-CHARGE
George Kewin, AIA
Richard Rosson, AIA

PROJECT ARCHITECTS
Donna Barry, Greg Lynn,
Michael McInturf, Joseph Walter

PROJECT TEAM
Lawrence Blough, John Curran,
John Durschinger,
Martin Felsen, Kelly Hopkin,
Gregory Luhan, Marisabel Marratt,
John Maze, Edward Mitchell,
Maureen Murphy Ochsner,
Astrid Perlbinder, Jerome Scott,
Jim Wilson, Brad Winkeljohn

PROJECT ASSISTANTS
Arcand Arnold, Andrew Burmeister,
Vincent Costa, Reid Freeman,
John Garra, Nazli Gonensay,
Martin Houston, Mathew Jogan,
Richard Labonte, Heidi McCahan,
Elizabeth Muske, Corrine Nacinovic,
Jean-Gabriel Neukomn, Joseph Ostrafi,
Karen Pollock, Jim Wilson,
Jason Winstanley, Sarah Whiting,
Leslie Young

ASSOCIATE ARCHITECT
Lorenz & Williams, Inc.

PRINCIPAL-IN-CHARGE
Richard Roediger, AIA

PROJECT TEAM
Larry Anderson, James Harrell,
Jerome Flynn, Michael Downing,
B.H. Jon, Joseph Mitlo,
Shari Rethman, James Schriefer,
Michael Schuyler

CONSULTANTS

COST ESTIMATOR
Dugan & Meyers, Inc.

CIVIL ENGINEER
United Consultants
Banwo Longe

LANDSCAPE ARCHITECT
Hargreaves Associates
George Hargreaves, Glenn Allen

STRUCTURAL, MECHANICAL, PLUMBING, ELECTRICAL ENGINEER
Progressive Engineering
Timothy Raberding (engineering manager), Lester Picker, Ashok Patel, Scott Moniaci, Ali Hooshiari, Roger Butler, Paul Roush, Mike Blake, Elizabeth Lisac, Tim McCrate, Phil Miller

ACOUSTICAL
Jaffe Acoustics
Mark Holden

LIGHTING
Fisher Marantz
Richard Renfro

AUDIO VISUAL
Boyce Nemec Designs
Andy Smith

COLOR CONSULTANT
Donald Kaufman Color
Donald Kaufman

PHOTOGRAPHY
Dick Frank Studios (models)
Jeff Goldberg/ESTO (building)
Maureen France (construction and building, pg. 158), Anne Glenn (construction)

CONTRACTORS

CONSTRUCTION MANAGER
Dugan & Meyers
Construction Company
Francis Dugan (CEO)
Jerome Meyers (President)
Daniel Dugan (project manager)
Andy Englehart, Pete Kauffman,
Steve Klinker, Eric Kohls,
Patricia Purtee, Charlie Simon,
Julie Tolliver

CONSTRUCTION LAYOUT
Woolpert Consultants
Leo R. Flischel (Partner)
Marty McClain (project manager)
Tom Baumann

ELECTRICAL CONTRACTOR
Ayer Electric, Inc.
Donald Ayer (President)
Chris McKee (project manager)
Ralph Jump, Jr.

CONCRETE CONTRACTOR
Baker Concrete Construction, Inc.
Daniel Baker (President)

MECHANICAL CONTRACTOR
Cincy Mechanicals, Inc.
James A. Stetter (President)
Tom Swope (project manager)
Wendel Hofmann

GENERAL TRADES CONTRACTOR
Cleveland Construction Company, Inc.
Mark T. Small (Senior Vice President)
John Zeller (project manager)
Rhett Stayer

FIRE PROTECTION CONTRACTOR
Dalmatian Fire, Inc.
Bob Tansy (Vice President)
Dave Martin

STRUCTURAL CONTRACTOR
Danis Building Construction Company
Thomas P. Hammelrath (President)
Dave Daniel and Kevin Cozart (project managers), Butch Chewning

PLUMBING CONTRACTOR
Thomas J. Dyer Company
Thomas Grote, Jr. (President)
Tom Burr (project manager)
Steve NeCamp

CONTRIBUTORS TO THE
ARONOFF CENTER FOR DESIGN AND ART

The Dorothy and Lawson Reed Gallery
Gift of Mrs. C. Lawson Reed, Cincinnati

The Dr. Stanley and Mickey Kaplan Auditorium
Gift of Dr. Stanley and Mickey (DAAP 1950)
Kaplan, Cincinnati

Lynne Meyers Gordon Commemorative Gift Fund
Gift of Lynne Meyers Gordon (DAAP 1986) in
memory of her father, Philip Mitchell Meyers, Sr.,
and brother, Philip Mitchell Meyers, Jr.

Office, public space, and studio furniture
Gift of Knoll, Inc., New York City

Drafting tables and furniture
Gift of Skidmore, Owings & Merrill, New York City

CONTRIBUTORS TO
ELEVEN AUTHORS IN SEARCH OF A BUILDING

Printing
The Hennegan Company, Cincinnati, Ohio

Paper
Mead Fine Papers, Dayton, Ohio

4,000 copies of this book
were printed by
The Hennegan Company on
Mead 80lb Signature Dull.

The principal typeface is
Bell Gothic, designed by
C. H. Griffith in 1938.

The book was designed by
Michael Bierut and
Esther Bridavsky,
Pentagram, New York.

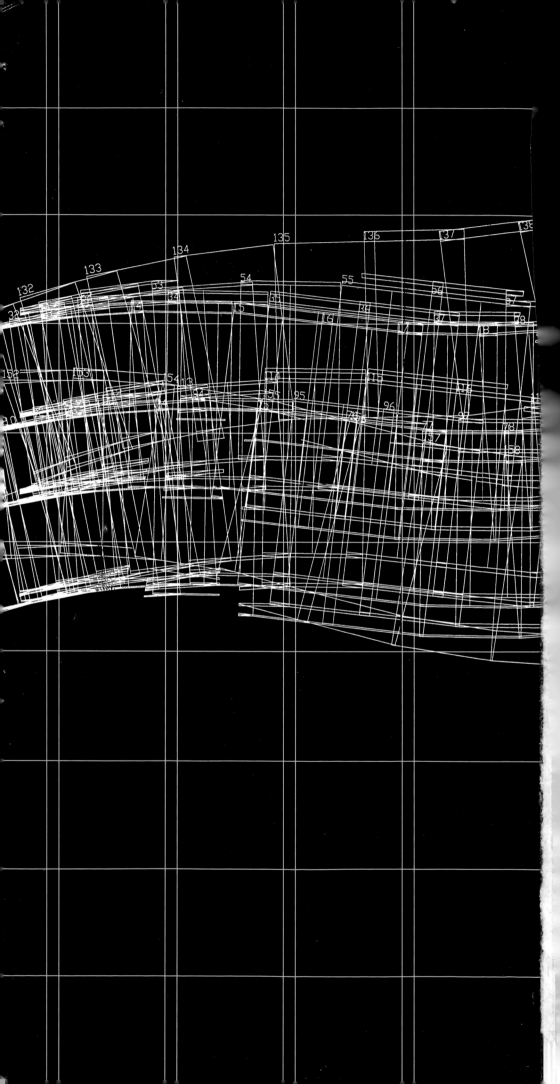